D1643002

FREE TO LOVE

A Manifesto
for Christian Freedom

Five Addresses Expounding Paul's Letter
to the Galatians

by
Trevor W. J. Morrow

To Carys

who has taught me to think clearly
and live authentically.

Contents

Foreword

by Archdeacon Ken Clarke

Few in Ireland today can match Trevor Morrow's deep understanding of a 1st century biblical Gospel and a 21st century British/Irish culture. Few have thought so rigorously, read so widely or listened so intently. He lives in the real world. The Rev. Dr. J.R.W. Stott's call to "double listening" (listening to God speaking in the Word and in the world) is seen and worked out so clearly in the teaching and preaching of the Rev. Dr. T.W.J. Morrow.

Since I first met Trevor in the 1960s, I have respected him for his radical, disciplined commitment to understand the Gospel, live by the Gospel, preach the Gospel and, with costly courage, apply the Gospel. This book is adequate proof of my observation. With his infectious enthusiasm and natural humour he unpacks Paul's letter to the Galatians. He exposes false loyalties. He challenges misunderstandings. He shatters misconceptions. He identifies empty cultural and religious traditions, distortions and perversions of the Gospel in Ireland today. He disturbs and unsettles – and what is his motivation? It is all for the sake of the Gospel which is the focus of Paul's letter to the Galatians. Trevor is teaching in the present what St. Paul taught in the past, and because it is God's Word we are uncomfortable.

One of St. Paul's concerns is that his hearers are not going on as God desires. They started well in their Christian lives, but something fundamental has gone wrong. One of the joys for all who know Trevor is to see him going on. In the face of the frustrations and anxieties of Christian leadership and the personal pressures and temptations unique to preachers, Trevor has kept going on. We have seen his potential realized. The promise of his younger years has been realized in faithful prophetic leadership at local and national level. God has blessed him with extraordinary gifts of preaching and teaching. Let no-one think they come easily. Prior to delivering the first of these Bible Readings at the 1999 New Horizon in Coleraine, Trevor was not only understandably apprehensive, but feeling utterly inadequate and physically sick. But out of natural weakness God wonderfully blesses. Trevor's life and ministry are a visual aid of the amazing grace he so often preaches and the Gospel of Jesus Christ which he so passionately proclaims. Out of love for the Lord, the Church and all on whom God's fingerprints are found, Trevor opens up the major themes of Galatians. The centrality of the Cross, the priority, power and purity of the Gospel, and the key issues of identity and integrity, so relevant to Christians in Ireland today, are just some of these themes.

I feel humbled to be asked to write this foreword. Thank you, Trevor. Reader, I have no hesitation in commending this book to you. Your heart will be warmed. Your mind will be stretched. Your soul will be nourished. Undoubtedly your life, attitudes and actions will change if you humbly and prayerfully read with this book in one hand and the Bible in the other.

May the Church in Ireland and the people of Ireland and beyond benefit from hearing God's Word through His servant, Trevor Morrow – an entertaining raconteur, a brave prophet, a compassionate pastor, a loyal friend, a committed family man . . . and above all a "Good News" man.

Ken Fanta Clarke

Preface

New Horizon, 1999, was a daunting and thrilling responsibility for me. I had never before attended this conference at the University of Ulster campus in Coleraine. It gathers thousands of Christians from all the denominations in Ireland for 'a balanced ministry of biblical teaching, of worship and praise of God and of challenge to service through the church.' My remit was to give five Bible readings. I chose to expound Paul's letter to the Galatians – his manifesto for Christian freedom.

It was during the preparation, but especially as I spoke, that the full implications of the Apostle Paul's direct and provocative message for Ireland began to emerge. For those who have lived through 'the troubles', this teaching is unsettling and liberating. It is quite clear from Paul's letter that 'justification by grace alone, through faith alone' is not only about the basis of our acceptance before God, but is also about the criteria which we use to accept one another as brothers and sisters in Christ. It is, therefore, pertinent to the times in which we live.

This little book is, in essence, the addresses given over those five mornings in August 1999. They have been transcribed and, through the skill and flair of Alison McCaughan, have been edited for publication. I am indebted to her because she has had to work at speed and with great grace. I am also grateful to everyone in the Publications Department in Church House who have ensured that all was ready in time. I also want to thank my good friend Archdeacon 'Fanta' Clarke for writing the foreword.

Trevor W. J. Morrow

"Do you know who I am?"

"No I don't, but if you ask the sister over there she'll tell you"

Freedom not Bondage

Galatians 1 vv.1-10

Let me begin with an urban myth. You know what urban myths are? They are stories that are passed on by word of mouth and they are told as if they are true because we know somebody who knows somebody who knows somebody to whom it has happened. Hence grannies are wrapped in carpets and carried from some part of Europe to Belfast or someone buys a peculiar dog in Spain and when he brings it home he discovers in fact that it's a rat – you've all heard these urban myths. Well this is an Ulster urban myth – I've heard it related so many times to Catholic cardinals to Presbyterian moderators to Baptist presidents, whatever. They are appearing in a formal capacity at an Old Peoples' Home. In front of them is one of the senior residents and the dignitary turns to this old lady and says to her, "Do you know who I am?" and she says, "No I don't, but if you ask the sister over there she'll tell you". That is an Ulster urban myth; I've heard it told so many times by so many different people. Of course it describes confusion. The Church in Ireland, and specifically the evangelical community, is at present in a state of confusion.

The time was when we knew who we were – being an evangelical Christian in Ulster was a package deal. You, of course, would be a Protestant and a unionist. You may not have had much money but you would certainly have embraced middle class values of what was respectable and decent in terms of what you wore and how you behaved. As a believer you, "did not smoke or drink or chew and did not go with girls who do". But now, "the times they are a-changin' ". You will find at this conference . . . I hope you find them . . . evangelical Roman Catholics who claim to be republicans. You could be sitting beside someone this morning who will have abandoned every principle of middle class Ulster evangelicalism because the underwear is no longer marked by the saintly Michael but by the saintly Bernard; no longer are evangelicals consistently total abstainers, so you could be at the prayer meeting with someone who is a paid up member of the 'Sunday Times' Wine Club. That's the way it is; "the times they are a-changin' ". Nevertheless, as parents, we know that our children are living in a moral jungle. You and I fear for their safety, their survival and their very souls. Body, soul and spirit are all under threat. To be healthy or happy or holy at the dawn of a new millennium is an enormous challenge to us all. We are confused in terms of our identity – who are we; and in terms of our morality, how are we to live? It is no wonder, therefore, that we are seeking for certainty at a time of such radical change. Yet, it is because of such a desire that we are in danger of embracing a different Gospel. It is for this reason that I want us to turn to Paul's letter to the Galatians, because this Church was also in a state of confusion. Let's look at Galatians chapter one verses one to ten.

Galatians 1:1-10

"Paul an apostle - not sent from men nor by man, but by Jesus Christ and God the Father, who raised him from the dead - and all the brothers with me,

To the churches in Galatia:

Grace and peace to you from God our Father and the Lord Jesus Christ, who gave himself for our sins to rescue us from the present evil age, according to the will of our God and Father, to whom be glory for ever and ever. Amen.

I am astonished that you are so quickly deserting the one who called you by the grace of Christ and are turning to a different Gospel - which is really no Gospel at all. Evidently some people are throwing you into confusion and are trying to pervert the Gospel of Christ. But even if we or an angel from Heaven should preach a gospel other than the one we preach to you, let him be eternally condemned! As we have already said, so now I say again: if anybody is preaching to you a gospel other than that which you accepted, let him be eternally condemned!

Am I now trying to win the approval of men, or of God? Or am I trying to please men? If I were still trying to please men, I would not be a servant of Christ."

First of all, many of you will be aware that there is an endless controversy as to who are the recipients of this letter. Is it northern Galatia, which would mean that the letter is addressed to the Gauls or the Celts in what is now Turkey? It would be marvellous if it were so, because we could then apply the Word of God to those who are Scots and Welsh and Irish and ignore the English! My own feeling is that it is more certainly addressed to the Roman province of Galatia, which means that the churches who received this letter are the churches that Paul established on his first missionary journey recorded in Acts, chapters thirteen and fourteen. You recall how, after prayer and the laying on of hands, Paul and Barnabas leave Antioch and head off to the island of Cyprus; then to Derbe, Lystra, Iconium and Pisidian Antioch – the churches of Galatia. Now when Paul preaches the gospel, there is such unction upon his ministry that not only Jews but Gentiles receive the gospel and they do so with ecstasy, with such joy that it was as if Paul were an angel from Heaven. But now something has happened to this church. Verse seven says, **"They are troubled and confused."** Evidently, Paul states, some people are throwing you into confusion and trying to pervert the gospel of Christ. Now that word for "confusion" is the same word used to describe the disciples in the boat when the storm is raging and to describe Herod when he hears that a new king has been born. It is a description of someone who is emotionally unsettled, frightened, upset, confused. Now what is happening here? Well simply, the Galatians are deserting the gospel.

You will note that on five occasions in just a matter of a few verses, Paul mentions the word "gospel" - **"I am astonished you are turning to a different *gospel* . . . it is really no *gospel* at all . . . there are those trying to pervert the *gospel* of Christ . . . If we or an angel should preach a *gospel* other than the one we preach, let them be eternally condemned. If anyone is preaching to you a *gospel* other than that which you accepted, let him be eternally condemned".** If there is anything we are to grasp from this paragraph, it is the importance of the teaching of doctrine, of *apostolic gospel*. Now it is crucial for us in this generation to emphasize such an element in our faith because, according to Neil Postman in his classic work, it is not just in the world, but in the Church, that we are "amusing ourselves to death". I don't know how many of you have seen Episode One of "Star Wars"; I have seen it on a big, massive screen of a cinema that has just been opened in Dublin. It's not a great movie, but it's extremely entertaining. There is one moment where Liam Neeson as Qui-Gon Jinn turns to this young boy who will be the father of Luke Skywalker – if you are familiar with all the other episodes – and at this critical moment just before this race begins, he says to him "Don't think. *Feel*; and may the force be with you". Well isn't that the essence of much evangelical Christianity that we are confronted with today? Don't think. Feel; and may the power be with you.

Do you know the story of the debate which took place between the theologian and the astronomer? The astronomer said, "I get really irritated by you theologians talking about the epistemic correlations within the hypostatic union - or you debating justification and sanctification and the using of those profound theological terms. For me the gospel is quite simple, 'Jesus loves me - this I know, for the bible tells me so'." And the theologian said, "Well, yes, I understand what you're saying. I respond in exactly the same manner to astronomers when they talk about exploding novae and galactical perturbations and black holes. When I look at the heavens it is simply, 'Twinkle, twinkle little star, how I wonder what you are'."   We've got to THINK. Cliff Morgan tells this lovely story which happened at an all-important moment during the final of a British Lions Tour of South Africa. A second row forward (you know second row forwards - they are all brawn and no brains . . . I was a second row forward) who was an Irishman, grabbed the ball and did something absolutely outrageous with it and Cliff Morgan said to him, "Think man, think!" And he replied, "How can I think and shove at the same time?" And some of you wonder how you can think and believe at the same time. Well, you've got to think. You've got to understand the gospel; you've got to embrace the gospel because our failure to do so is the source of confusion in the Church today just as it was in the Church in Galatia. So quickly, says Paul, so easily you are deserting the gospel. This is the picture, is it not, of Moses having gone up to Mount Sinai to receive the law of God and when he returns he is astounded that the children of Israel, who have been redeemed from enslavement, should now be worshipping an Egyptian fertility god and deserting the God of their fathers. If you're a school teacher you know what it's like. You leave a classroom for a few moments and you say to the children, "I want you to behave; I've just a little errand to do," and when you come back - what is going on? Anarchy, chaos, paper airplanes are being thrown, hair is being pulled and chairs have been overthrown. Paul is astounded that, so quickly, these people are deserting the gospel that he preached . . . and is he angry? People have read this language and see this as pure pique, but I think not! Look at chapter four, versus nineteen and twenty. He says, **"My dear children, for whom I am again in the pains of childbirth until Christ is formed in you, how I wish I could be with you now and change my tone because I am perplexed about you."** He is baffled, astounded, perplexed, that the Galatians are turning against him, they are turning against the gospel and even, more seriously, they are turning against God himself. Well, what is happening here?

Certain trouble makers and agitators have entered the Church. These are the authors of the confusion; it is possible that they are from Jerusalem and they are certainly Jews. Their argument goes something like this. "We believe the gospel. We believe that Jesus is Messiah, that He is the Saviour of the world. But it is not enough just to believe in Jesus Christ. Something else is required in order to be acceptable before God and to be acceptable to each other within the community of faith. It is necessary also to become a Jew; you must be circumcised;

you must eat only kosher food; you must keep the food laws and celebrate the special holy days". These people, you see, are appalled at the abandonment of their Jewish identity, so they are saying, "Listen, the gospel is true . . . but something else is needed". Now to establish their thesis, it is necessary for them to turn their guns against the Apostle Paul and against his gospel. So as far as Paul is concerned these agitators are saying, "Listen, Paul has no real authority to preach like this; he's not a real apostle; he was not with the twelve. He has no sanction from headquarters, from '*mother Church*' in Jerusalem . . . and anyway, isn't he just a man pleaser? The gospel he preaches is so easy. He goes to these Gentiles and says that all you have to do is to receive the free grace of God in Jesus Christ by faith alone. It's too easy. He is seducing these people; he is winning his converts by abandoning the obligations of the law". Now in response to this confusion and to these troublemakers Paul writes his letter to the Galatians. Timothy George says, "Galatians bristles with passion, sarcasm and anger". Richard Longenecker writes, "It is like a lion turned loose in the arena of Christianity". So let me tell you from the outset that this book is provocative, blunt and direct; but I am speaking mostly to Ulster men and women so this ought not be a problem. After all, this is our style.

Paul is not a man pleaser and this can be seen in two ways. The first is the very structure of the letter itself. When we write letters we normally put our address on the top right hand corner or in the centre. If it's a

formal letter we'll have the name and address of the
recipient on the left hand corner, the date and then we
begin, "Dear Fred, Dear Mary, I'm so sorry that it's so
long since I last wrote". My letters usually begin like
that. But within this culture, letters were structured
in a totally different way. Paul follows the Hellenistic
pattern of letter writing. He begins with the author,
Paul, an apostle, sent by God, not from headquarters
mother church (we'll come to that in a moment) and
then he mentions the recipients, the Galatians, we think
churches like Pisidian Antioch. There follow the
greetings, "Grace and peace". Now at this point in all of
Paul's letters and according to Hellenistic culture there
ought to be a thanksgiving. If you know anything about
the Middle East, you will realise it is essential before
you begin to engage in any business that you affirm
the people to whom you are relating. That is part of
their culture. You honour them, you respect them, their
family, their relations, the contribution that they have
made - even to the point of flattery. Now in all of
Paul's letters he follows that pattern. In his letter to
the Romans and in all his other letters Paul says, "Hey
folks, you're great, your faith is being reported all over
the world. I give thanks for every remembrance of you."
But when he writes to the Galatians there is no
thanksgiving. He is straight into the theme; he goes
immediately for the jugular and notice the tone of his
rebuke. This is stern stuff. Look at verses eight and
nine - **"If we or an angel from heaven should preach a
gospel other than the one we preached to you, let him
be cursed, anathematized, condemned. If anybody is**

preaching to you a gospel other than the one that you have accepted, let him be cursed, anathematized, condemned." Eugene Peterson says that cursing - before it degenerated into mere profanity - was noble religious speech. "Genesis records the first curses; the serpent was cursed to eat dust; woman was cursed with pain in childbirth; man was cursed with toil; the ground was cursed with thorns and thistles. So," says Peterson, "Paul continues the venerable practice and pronounces a vigorous double curse on persons who pervert the life of gospel freedom." What Paul is doing here, is that he is exercising the ministry of a prophet. When a prophet came, he either came pronouncing benediction and he would say, "Blessed, blessed," or he came to curse and to condemn in the name of God. Remember that this is the ministry - the *prophetic* ministry of Jesus Christ. He said, **"Blessed are you Simon . . ." ; "Blessed are you who mourn . . . Blessed are you who hunger and thirst after righteousness."** And Christ also exercised the prophetic ministry of cursing; He said, **"Woe to you Korazin and Bethsaida"; "Woe to you scribes and Pharisees"**. In exactly the same way Paul pronounces the curse upon these troublemakers. **"So,"** says Paul, **"am I now trying to win the approval of men, or of God? If I write like this and speak like this, am I a man pleaser? If I were still trying to please men I would not be a servant of Christ."**

Who are these troublemakers? What are they doing? Why are they doing it? Why do they create such a reaction from the apostle? Well let's stand back for a moment to understand what is going on here. The assumptions of all Jews, as the children of Abraham, was that the promise to Abraham of cosmic salvation would take place through Judaism; that all the ends of the earth would experience the salvation of God. So the prophet Isaiah speaks in these terms, **"I will make you a light for the Gentiles that you may bring my salvation to the ends of the earth, that the earth might be filled with the knowledge of God as the water covers the sea."** Now the expectation of the Jews was that this would be accomplished through Judaism; it was the primary motivation of their proselytising activity. Some of you will remember that just a few years ago during the Ethiopian conflict over Eritrea, that Israel brought out great numbers of black, African Falasha Jews. They are not Semitic Jews and they could not trace their lineage from Abraham. They were the subject of proselytizing - part of the Jewish vision of the universal reign of God through Judaism. Now the early Church was Jewish. Its headquarters was Jerusalem and the early believers recognized Jesus as the Messiah. The missionary strategy of the Church was initially to Jews and God fearers and was therefore based on their synagogues. But two things happened in the early Church that totally blew apart the thinking of many of those Christians who were Jews, including the apostle Paul.

Here is the first one and it happened on the first missionary journey. It was the conversion of the pro-consul of Pathos in Cyprus, Sergius Paulus. You

remember he requested an audience with Paul and
Barnabas. However, Bar-Jesus, a Jewish magician
strongly objected to this. So Paul confronts him; he is
temporarily blinded and eventually Sergius Paulus
believes the gospel. Now what is the significance of
that? Well, here is a Gentile who comes to faith without
any reference to Judaism. He is not one of the God-
fearers. He has never been part of the synagogue . . .
and yet he receives Jesus as Messiah and as Saviour.
Now I believe that has a profound effect upon the whole
strategy of mission for the early Church. Combine that
with the gospel, which Paul received - he received it in
Arabia where he was probably meditating and reflecting
upon the purposes of God. If you want to know what
he received, look at Ephesians chapter three, verses two
following. This is an extraordinary statement for
someone who had been trained by Rabbi Gamaliel in
historic Judaism. **"Surely,"** he says, **"You have heard
about the administration of God's grace that was given
to me for you, that is the mystery made known to me
by revelation as I have already written briefly. In
reading this you will be able to understand my insight
into the mystery of Christ which was not made known
to men in other generations as it is now being revealed
by the Spirit to God's holy apostles and prophets. This
mystery is that through the gospel the Gentiles are
heirs together with Israel, members together of one
body and sharers together in the promise in Christ
Jesus."** From this point, from the conversion of Sergius
Paulus, from the revelation that the apostle Paul receives
in Arabia, the whole strategy of the early Church is

transformed. Gentiles are to be received into the fellowship of the community of God's people without them becoming Jews.

Now you can imagine the response of many of these Christian Jews. They are startled. I assure you they are far from being happy and some of them are absolutely furious. Some of them come down from Jerusalem to sort out the church in Galatia. Who are they? Let me say from the outset that I believe they are Christians in the sense that they believe the basics of the faith; they would have had no difficulty reciting the Apostles' Creed: 'I believe in God the Father Almighty, Maker of heaven and earth and in Jesus Christ His only son Our Lord, conceived by the Holy Spirit, born of the Virgin Mary, suffered under Pontius Pilot, crucified dead and buried . . .' and so on. They could have publicly made such a profession. Therefore the problem which Paul faced here in the church in Galatia was not liberalism in the church. It was not that these people had abandoned the supernatural dimensions of the faith or of revealed religion; they did not question the deity of Christ or his Messiahship; they had no problems with the Trinity of God or a blood atonement. They believed the foundations, the fundamentals of the faith. It is for this reason that I believe this book specifically addresses two groups of people in Ireland at this time.

The first is the Roman Catholic Church and the second - which may be more startling to those who are present - is evangelical Protestantism. They are, if you like, the two branches that are still within Christendom desperately holding on to essential elements of historic catholicity. Today these two groupings in Ireland are concerned with exactly the same two issues which were confronting the agitators in Galatia. Concern number one is religious identity : who are we?. Number two is moral integrity: how are we to behave?

The first question is one that we struggle with in this country all the time. In some senses it lies at the heart of the political traumas which have been confronting us for generations. Do you know the story of the two women sitting in a bus in Belfast? A man and woman are sitting in front of them and this woman turns to the other and says, "Them pair are going to get married." "No," says the other. "Oh yes - and she's one of them and he walks". Now, that's all about identity - Who am I?

Nothing was more important for the Jew than who they were . . . they were God's people. They perceived themselves in those terms and they knew they were God's people because they bore the mark of circumcision, the sign and seal of the covenant and they kept the Torah, the law of God and that was what made them a special people. So, contrary to many opinions, I do not believe these agitators were saying "We are saved by merely keeping the law". What they were saying was that it is important to believe in Jesus Christ but it is also necessary to become as we are in order to be acceptable before God and to be acceptable to each other.

Bruce Longenecker in an extraordinarily good book called 'The Triumph of Abraham's God' says this, "The agitators' case would have followed along these lines. Having enjoyed God's initial acceptance in Christ, the Gentile Christians now needed to be brought into full membership with God's covenant people by observing the practices of the law that marked out ethnic Israel. The question that concerned the Galatian Christians, then, was not so much, 'How can I get saved? By works or by faith?' Instead their interests were focused on the identity of the people of God and whether God's blessing could be fully enjoyed without observing the stipulations laid out in the scriptures given by God to Israel." Now, combine those theological convictions with a phenomenon which we are aware of – a growing nationalism. Listen to these comments by Robert Jewett, "There was at this time a resurgence of zealot activity in Judea under the governor Tiberius Julius Alexander, (AD46 to 48) who crucified two insurgent leaders, and during this period of office disorder increased. Zealot vengeance was liable to be visited on Jews who fraternised with Gentiles and Jewish Christians, who shared table fellowship with their fellow Gentile brethren, were also exposed to such reprisals. If Gentile Christians could be persuaded to accept circumcision this, it was hoped, would protect Jewish Christians against zealot vengeance. You see, at a time of rampant Jewish nationalism, Jewish Christians thought that if these Gentiles could only became part of the Jewish culture, it would also protect them because they could convey to the zealots that they were actually the same people. Such was the passionate craving for identity and also, of course, for moral integrity.

It was inconceivable for the Jews that they would not keep the Torah, the law. During the famous discourse between Justin Martyr and Trypho the Jew, Trypho the Jew urges Justin along these lines. "First, be circumcised; then keep as the law commands relating to the Sabbath, the feasts and God's new moons and, in a word, do all the things that are written in the law and then you will indeed find mercy from God." Well, you and I can understand the concerns of these Jewish Christians. The implication seemed to be that if you simply believed in Jesus Christ, you didn't have to keep the law - you could do whatever you liked. The Jewish Christians were horrified by this. That is why their influence was so subtle and insidious, so that even Barnabas was taken in - even the apostle Peter. All of us feel the recognition and requirement at times for some form of law, especially if we have children. The first time Carys, my wife, and I left our pair, (they're 22 and 21 now, so this is quite a few years ago), we left them as teenagers in the house for about a week. I prepared Dad's ten commandments which were clearly posted up in the kitchen and they had to be observed - all sorts of rules, some of them quite easy, like making sure that they watered plants or that they locked doors. Rule number 10 was; no members of the opposite sex in your room after 10 o'clock. Now we all feel the necessity, do we not, to establish such rules and regulations. It is out of a genuine concern. So what happens when young

Christians come into the church? We say, "It's wonderful that you are a Christian, that you are now following Jesus Christ - here are the laws; here are the rules for you to be accepted in here; this is what you have to do." That's what we do and there are reasons for it. Yes, we can identify with this behaviour, not only because we are concerned for the moral wellbeing of these young Christians, but also because we are increasingly confronted by a clash of civilisations, a craving for identity and the re-emergence of nationalism. This we can all see, for example, throughout eastern Europe with the disintegration of totalitarian communism.

We can distinguish between what we call ethnic nationalism and civil nationalism. Civil nationalism says that everyone who is born here belongs here. Ethnic nationalism says everything that is the same as me (that is, the same as us) belongs here. It is not civil but ethnic nationalism which has led to the conflagration in the Balkans. All of those ethnic groups which were somehow restrained during various empires and under Tito himself - Croatians, Slovenians, Bosnians, Serbs, Macedonians, Montenegrans, Kosovars, all of them were somehow held in check. But now they are in tension and conflict with each other because of the craving for identity. It also lies at the root of the Middle East problem, does it not? Culture, ethnicity, religion and a desire to hold onto a portion of land are woven together; and, of course, we in Ireland recognize it too.

I don't know what you think of Conor Cruise O'Brien, the 'Cruiser' as he's known in Dublin. Whatever you think of his politics he is one of the great wordsmiths of the century. Anything that he writes is a delight to read. Two of his works, 'God-Land: Reflections on Religion and Nationalism' and, perhaps his more popular, 'Ancestral Voices' give us an amazing insight into the weaving together of religion and nationalism in this country. In the pursuit of identity, says Conor Cruise O'Brien, in the pursuit of Irish nationalism, particularly in the 19th century, there was a major cleavage between the Church and the republican cause. But under the guidance of Cardinal Paul Cullen a passion for Irishness, Catholicity and national identity began to be woven together and have become so deeply ingrained into the psyche of Irish men and women in this generation that they are virtually inseparable. So, in most parts of the world, if you say that you are Irish, they assume you are Catholic, even though almost 20% of the population of this island is not Catholic. Of course in response to all of this, Ulster Protestants have pursued their own identity. The weaving together of cultural inheritance, ethnicity, political aspiration, religious conviction all over a portion of land . . . the same phenomenon that is repeated throughout this world, is here among us, and so you and I seek the answer to the question in this context, "Who am I?"

Add to this the moral disintegration of our culture, the sex scandals within the Church, the condition of the society in which our children have to live, and it's not surprising that we all feel confused. As an example of the problems in society, consider this. It comes from the United States, but I think it is equally applicable in our situation. Here is a survey of American High School Principals in 1958. They were asked, "What are the main problems among your students?" The answers were:-

1. Not doing homework.
2. Not respecting property, for example, throwing books.
3. Leaving lights on and doors and windows open.
4. Throwing spit balls in class (you can just imagine what they are!).
5. Running through the halls.

If you are teaching today this is dreamland. In 1988 a similar survey was carried out amongst the Principals of the same High Schools; "What are the main problems among your students?"

1. Abortion
2. Aids
3. Rape
4. Drugs
5. Fear of violent death, murder and guns and knives in school.

It is no wonder that we seek not only identity, but that we yearn for a sense of moral certainty. We crave for symbols and standards to show who we are and how we are to live. It is because of this that we are in danger of embracing a different gospel.

The Apostle Paul is adamantly opposed to all such legal obligation with regard to identity and integrity for these three reasons:-

First, he sees the consequences for the fellowship and mission of the Church. If the principles of these agitators are embraced, the Church of God will become ethnically and culturally bound. Remember the early Church is a Jewish phenomenon, but the vision the apostle Paul has is of a cosmic, universal Church - men and women from every nation, tribe and tongue. The implications are clear; if your community or fellowship is bound by one of this island's cultures or sub-cultures then you are not in step with the mission of Christ's Church in this place. For example, Lucan church, where I minister, was founded by Scots in the 19th century - Scotsmen who came to be the stewards of various estates and to help run the mills situated on the River Liffey. Now can you imagine what would happen if we, in Lucan, decided that the wearing of kilts was to be a prerequisite for Sunday morning worship - that everybody had to do it, because that's who we are; that's our Scottish heritage; that's the tradition of our forefathers; that's where we want to stand . . . and better still, we are Presbyterians. But in principle that is no different from putting a flag outside our building and saying, 'This is who we are". When we do this we become ethnically and culturally bound in terms of our identity, and it can sound the death knell for mission in this country. I feel this with such passion because I have been a missionary for the past sixteen and a half years in a different culture from my inheritance. Everything that I have and am is committed to the coming of the kingdom of God throughout this island. Whatever the cultural background, whatever the political aspiration, whatever the denominational allegiance of men and women, I want to see the kingdom come; but to practise the principles of the Galatian agitators would be to disempower the Church of Jesus Christ. And we have done it in this country. Let me put it even more directly; if I understand the Apostle Paul correctly, to envelope a crucifix in a Tricolour is another gospel: to wrap the cross of Christ in the Union Jack is another gospel. I can put it no more bluntly than that.

The second reason for Paul opposing this so adamantly is that to go down the path of these agitators is to create moral and spiritual bondage. Yes, they have high motives; they are fearful for righteousness and for the integrity of the people; so are the people of the country we live in. When they see the decadence of our society, no wonder they want to impose rigorous laws upon Christian people in order to preserve some standards of right and wrong. But Paul will not have it. He wants us to be liberated from such oppression. One of my Catholic friends gave me a marvellous book. If you're from a Catholic background I suggest you read this; it is hilarious. It's called 'Growing up Catholic'. It's really a description of pre-Vatican II Catholicism in Boston and of what it means to live under law. What sort of 'laws' operated? Well, if you were at a baseball game on a Friday night and you wanted a hot dog, you had a problem because you are not supposed to eat meat on Friday. "Now just considering eating meat on Friday is a venial sin; wanting to eat meat is another one. So you have not even moved in your seat and you have already sinned twice. What if you actually ate one?! Aside from the risk of choking on forbidden food and receiving your temporal punishment on the spot, have you committed a mortal sin or a venial sin? Well, if you think it's mortal, it may be mortal; and if you think it's venial, it may still may be mortal. After much thought you decide it's venial, so you call the hot dog vendor, you take the money out of your pocket and you buy a hot dog; this is clearly an act of free will. You figure you can go to confession on Saturday - but wait, does a venial sin become mortal when you commit it deliberately? That's a chance you take. What if you've forgotten it's Friday? In that case eating the hot dog may not be a sin . . . but forgetting that it's Friday is! What if you remember that it's Friday half way through the hot dog, is it a venial sin to finish it? If you throw it away, is wasting food a sin? Within five minutes you have committed enough sins to land you in purgatory for a million years! The simplest course is just not to take any chances, avoid the near occasion of sin and stay out of the ball park on Fridays." Now those of you who are Protestants may think, "Well isn't it great not to be like that?" But ladies, don't you remember all the struggles you've had as to how much powder you should put on your face - just enough to take away the shine or a little more to enhance your beauty? You know you could be entering an arena, a church, where a preacher will be yelling and screaming at you, "You Jezebels!!! You have enough paint to paint a battleship and enough powder to blow it up!" - and you will have to sit there and cringe. Remember all the struggles you've had within this evangelical sub-culture? You could wear earrings if they were studs . . . but not danglies. Studs are in, danglies are out – who says? Who is making all these rules? Who are these people? At least the Catholic Church has the magesterium making their decisions. Who is deciding for us? And so we find ourselves trapped in the same legal and moral bondage. Well, let me tell you, Paul's letter to the Galatians is a cry for freedom. He will not have it.

Finally, and perhaps most important of all, Paul won't have it because it is a denial of the gospel. Look at verses six to ten. In fact, if you want to know what Paul's understanding of the gospel is, just look very briefly at verses three to five; **"Grace and peace to you from God our Father and the Lord Jesus Christ, who gave Himself for our sins to rescue us from the present evil age, according to the will of our God and Father, to whom be glory for ever and ever".** Well, we understand that Christ gave Himself for our sins - that there is something about the cross which unleashes power in dealing with the problems of moral rebellion. But when it comes to the next phrase, we somehow miss the point because this is a challenge to the craving for identity. What Paul says here about, **'rescuing us from the present evil age'** is the language of Ezekiel and Daniel. He perceives that this present age of sin and death will run its course and end in judgement. The new age will be inaugurated by the coming of Messiah in the clouds of glory and in the resurrection of the dead, the bringing of Satan into submission and in the coming of the reign of peace; and this is the vision of the Old Testament prophets. Now here is the point; Jesus is the Messiah who was crucified for our sins – and for that reason, as the resurrected Christ, He has already inaugurated the new age. This is the mystery that has been revealed to the apostle Paul - that all things that have been vitiated and broken through sin will be restored and brought to harmony in Jesus Christ. What things? Things like the ethnic distinctions between Jews and Gentiles, between republicans and loyalists, between Kosovars and Serbs; the social barriers of slave and free; the gender wars of male and female, all of these are brought into unity in Jesus Christ; this is the new age. To try and hold on to an ethnic or political identity as an addition to the gospel is to *preach another gospel*, and furthermore, it is to try and make us live in the age of sin and death, when in fact, as Christians, we are a new creation. Have you grasped that? We are the children of the age which is to come. The old has gone; the new has come. This is our primary identity; we are the sons of God.

"And that's the way it is, Goodnight".
Walter Cronkite, CBS

Authentic not Counterfeit

Galatians 1 v.11 – 2 v.21

This is it; this is the real thing.

In this address we are going to look at Galatians 1 v. 11 to the end of chapter 2.

"I want you to know, brothers, that the gospel I preached is not something man made up I did not receive it from any man, nor was I taught it; rather, I received it by revelation from Jesus Christ.

For you have heard of my previous way of life in Judaism, how intensely I persecuted the church of God and tried to destroy it. I was advancing in Judaism beyond many Jews of my own age and was extremely zealous for the traditions of my fathers. But when God, who set me apart from birth and called me by His grace, was pleased to reveal His Son in me so that I might preach Him among the Gentiles, I did not consult any man, nor did I go up to Jerusalem to see those who were apostles before I was, but I went immediately into Arabia and later returned to Damascus.

Then after three years, I went up to Jerusalem to get

acquainted with Peter and stayed with him fifteen days. I saw none of the other apostles – only James, the Lord's brother. I assure you before God that what I am writing to you is no lie. Later I went to Syria and Cilicia. I was personally unknown to the churches of Judea that are in Christ. They only heard the report: "The man who formerly persecuted us is now preaching the faith he once tried to destroy." And they praised God because of me.

Fourteen years later I went up again to Jerusalem, this time with Barnabas. I took Titus along also. I went in response to a revelation and set before them the gospel that I preach among the Gentiles. But I did this privately to those who seemed to be leaders, for fear that I was running or had run my race in vain. Yet not even Titus, who was with me, was compelled to be circumcised, even though he was a Greek. This matter arose because some false brothers had infiltrated our ranks to spy on the freedom we have in Christ Jesus and to make us slaves. We did not give in to them for a moment, so that the truth of the gospel might remain with you.

As for those who seemed to be important – whatever they were makes no difference to me; God does not judge by external appearance – those men added nothing to my message. On the contrary, they saw that I had been entrusted with the task of preaching the gospel to the Gentiles, just as Peter had been to the Jews. For God, who was at work in the ministry of

Peter as an apostle to the Jews, was also at work in my ministry as an apostle to the Gentiles. James, Peter and John, those reputed to be pillars, gave me and Barnabas the right hand of fellowship when they recognised the grace given to me. They agreed that we should go to the Gentiles, and they to the Jews. All they asked was that we should continue to remember the poor, the very thing I was eager to do.

When Peter came to Antioch, I opposed him to his face, because he was clearly in the wrong. Before certain men came from James, he used to eat with the Gentiles. But when they arrived, he began to draw back and separate himself from the Gentiles because he was afraid of those who belonged to the circumcision group. The other Jews joined him in his hypocrisy, so that by their hypocrisy even Barnabas was led astray.

When I saw that they were not acting in line with the truth of the gospel, I said to Peter in front of them all, "You are a Jew, yet you live like a Gentile and not like a Jew. How is it, then, that you force Gentiles to follow Jewish customs?

"We who are Jews by birth and not 'Gentile sinners' know that a man is not justified by observing the law, but by faith in Jesus Christ. So we, too, have put our faith in Christ Jesus that we may be justified by faith in Christ and not by observing the law, because by observing the law no-one will be justified.

"If, while we seek to be justified in Christ, it becomes evident that we ourselves are sinners, does that mean that Christ promotes sin? Absolutely not! If I rebuild what I destroyed, I prove that I am a law-breaker. For through the law I died to the law so that I might live for God. I have been crucified with Christ and I no longer live, but Christ lives in me. The life I live in the body, I live by faith in the Son of God, who loved me and gave Himself for me. I do not set aside the grace of God, for if righteousness could be gained through the law, Christ died for nothing!"

Some of you will be familiar with the name of Walter Cronkite. He was the anchor man for the CBS evening news for many, many years in the United States of America and each evening he would conclude with his catch phrase, "And that's the way it is, Goodnight". Walter Cronkite was a modern man. A postmodern man, of course, would not speak in such terms. He would say something like, "Well, that's the way we see it," or, "That's the way it looks from here". It is you see, a reflection of what we call relativism. Ireland is a wonderful country to live in at this time, not least because of the growing tolerance and pluralism and that I believe is to be commended. But with this pluralism there is a rampant relativism where people will say to us, "There is no such thing as truth or falsehood; there is no such thing as right or wrong; you can't be sure about anything". Because of this I've taught our own young people in Lucan to respond in this way. When someone says to you, "You can't be sure of anything", you are to say to them, "Are you sure?" When they say to you, "There's no such thing as truth or falsehood," you are to say to them, "Is that true?" When they say, "There's no such thing as right or wrong", you are to say to them, "Is that right?" Relativism you see, is inherently self-contradictory but, because of it, we are shocked by the bluntness of the apostle Paul. For him there is a true gospel and a false gospel. There is right and wrong. There is good and bad and this, of course, is utterly alien to our contemporary culture. And yet for Paul, as the guardian, the custodian and the champion of grace, he delights in declaring that in Jesus Christ and His cross everything that is necessary for us has been accomplished; a glorious, a comprehensive salvation, entirely and completely by grace. No matter who you are, whether you are a Jew or a Gentile, a male or female, a slave or free, you are totally accepted in the presence of God on the basis of what Christ has done for us.

Now, we have discovered already that this message of grace was being challenged by some Judaisers, agitators who had entered the church in Galatia. In order to preserve their Jewish identity and to advocate what they saw as 'moral integrity', they thought it was necessary not only to believe in Jesus Christ as the Messiah and the Saviour of the world, but that it was also necessary to become a Jew, to be circumcised, to eat kosher food and to celebrate the special holy days. Paul, as we have discovered, would have none of this. In order to seek to refute the apostle Paul, the agitators' argument was twofold. Firstly, they argued, "Paul is not really an apostle; he is not one of the twelve; he was never with Jesus": and secondly they insisted, "This is not the teaching of 'mother Church' in Jerusalem". It is in response to this challenge that the apostle Paul sets out what I'm calling 'the real thing'.

First of all, Paul seeks to demonstrate from where he receives this gospel, that is its source or origin. Look at verses eleven and twelve. **"I want you to know brothers that the gospel I preached is not something that man made up. I did not receive it from any man, nor was I taught it; rather I received it by revelation from Jesus Christ."** This gospel, then, was not communicated to him literally by flesh and blood. I hope as you hear that, that it triggers within your memory bank the incident in Caesarea Philippi where Jesus says, **"Who do men say that I am?"** and the disciples respond, **"Some say you are John the Baptist, some say you are Elijah. But who do you say that I am?"** asks Jesus. Peter responds, **"You are the Christ, the Son of the living God,"** and Jesus says, **"Flesh and blood did not reveal this to you; this is a work of God".** You know the story of a Jewish rabbi, a Catholic priest and a Protestant minister discussing a particularly difficult issue and the Jewish rabbi said, "According to the Torah this is how we ought to behave," and the Catholic priest said, "According to the traditions of the Church, this is what is required," and the Protestant minister said, "Well it seems to me . . ." As far as Paul is concerned what he teaches is not an opinion, it is not a personal view and it is not a school of thought. This has been revealed from Jesus Christ.

Secondly, Paul speaks with genuine authority. Remember the trouble makers were saying, "Paul is a great convert to the faith; he is an outstanding evangelist, but he is not an apostle. He's not one of the inner group. He has no imprimatur from Jerusalem. Headquarters have not licensed him. They have not ordained him. They have not sanctioned his ministry." This is Paul's answer, "You're absolutely right. I did not receive my credentials from them; I did not consult with any of them; I did not go to their Bible training course and I did not attend their theological seminary. I went to Arabia and I prayed and studied for three years. Oh, I did go off and see Peter and James. I had a great relationship with them, but not long enough to be taught by them. I was just there for a fortnight, just fifteen days." Now Paul is not saying here that the gospel he preaches is different from the gospel which the other apostles preach; in fact he will seek to demonstrate that his message is the same as that of the apostles in Jerusalem. But what he is indicating is that he has received it independently from them. You see the question here is the question of authority. Where does authority reside? Now this is a vital question in the Church today because, as you know, the pendulum swings backwards and forwards. Certainly in pre-Vatican II days, the Catholic church was predominantly authoritarian and hierarchical, with the pope at the top, then cardinal, archbishops, bishops, priests, people.

As you were received into the sacramental life of the Church you placed your mind, your heart and your conscience under the authority of that Church. It determined your moral judgement and your spiritual life. Of course one of the dangers of the Reformation was that the reformers replaced one pope with thousands of them - and it's possible that you are ministered to by one of them. Let me assure you that those of us who handle the word of God find this to be an extraordinary danger. We are confronted, as ministers of the gospel, with people who are spiritually vulnerable; they are desperate to hear the word of God and they are so easily manipulated. Tragically, throughout the Irish Republic, numerous small groups have emerged where strong charismatic, authoritarian figures seek to dominate their people so that we have bruised and broken individuals, many of whom have found their way to our congregation in Lucan.

So what is the alternative to authoritarianism and spiritual anarchy? Well Paul tells us in this passage; the Church locally and universally sits under the gospel and not the other way round. That's the emphasis and theme of this passage. The final authority for the apostle Paul is not in Jerusalem and for us it is not in Rome or in Canterbury or in Geneva or in the General Assembly of the Presbyterian Church in Ireland. This is not where the final authority resides; rather it is in the gospel itself. Of course those in leadership must give order and structure to the Church, they must interpret and apply the word of God, but what makes us distinctively evangelical is this final authority of the word of God. I have not the slightest hesitation because of my convictions to give a positive response to the question, "Do you believe the scriptures of the Old and New Testaments to be the only infallible rule of faith and practice?" This is our final authority.

If this is so, what is its credibility? What makes it believable? Well, the answer the apostle Paul gives may surprise some but I think that what he says in this passage is that the gospel authenticates itself. You see we do not create truth for people to believe in. Instead we are confronted by the eternal power and deity of God so that all men everywhere are without excuse. As you become self-conscious you become God-conscious, but the reality of God in terms of his awesome greatness and holiness is so traumatic to us - so unsettling to us - that we engage in the classic psychological activity of repression. We cannot cope with Him. So what do we do? Paul says in his letter to the Romans, **"We suppress the truth in our self-righteousness and we create for ourselves an alternative God, an aspect of the creation that we can cope with."** Now what happens when we see the light of the knowledge of the glory of God in the face of Jesus Christ, when we are confronted by the reality of the gospel, is that we simply see things as they are. The light comes on and we say, "This is me. I have discovered who I am. I have discovered who God is. I have discovered the purpose of my existence". The gospel simply declares it as it is. That is why, when people are confronted by the truth of the gospel as the

Holy Spirit opens their minds and hearts, it captivates them, so that it is ultimately irresistible.

Are you familiar with the testimony of C. S. Lewis - of how he came to faith? He describes the captivating power of the gospel in these terms, "You must picture me alone," he says, "in that room in Magdalene. Night after night feeling, whenever my mind lifted even for a second from my work, the steady unrelenting approach of Him whom I so earnestly desired not to meet. That which I greatly feared had at last come upon me in the Trinity term of 1929. I gave in and admitted that God was God and knelt and prayed . . . perhaps that night the most dejected and reluctant convert in all England." Reluctant, you see, but yet for him irresistible.

Now the apostle Paul describes his own conversion in the same terms. His life is radically changed so that the gospel is authenticated in his experience. Who is Paul before his conversion? Well, he describes himself; ethnically he is a Jew, a protégé of the famous Jewish theologian Gamaliel. Religiously a bigot, he hated this sect within Judaism who believed that the Messiah had come, that they had crucified Him and that He was raised to the status of deity and now to be worshipped. Paul wanted to have them destroyed; he despised them. He pursued them like a bloodhound, breathing out threats, seeking to destroy them. Religiously, you see, Paul was a bigot. Nationalistically, he was a fanatic. He describes himself as full of zeal for the traditions of his fathers. Listen to Timothy George, one of the commentators; "It is significant that Paul uses the word 'zealous' to describe his persecuting activity against the Church. The word zeal is prominent in the Macabbean literature where it refers to those Jewish leaders who were willing to resort to the use of force in order to defend their homeland, its temple and the law against foreign intruders. Paul describes himself as a zealot nationalist." Of course he himself, as a rabbi, would not have taken up arms, but he stood by and carried the coats of those who were stoning Stephen to death, did he not? We can identify with this man, can we not? Ethnically a Jew, religiously a bigot, nationalistically a fanatic and all of this, he thought, was fine. He thought he was doing the will of God, until God did something to him. **"I was set apart from birth,"** he said, **"called by His grace and God revealed His son to me,"** so that this man is totally turned around and the truth of the gospel is not only authenticated in his life but it is authenticated horizontally in terms of his relationships with others. Formerly he had despised the Gentiles; now he is an apostle to the Gentiles . . . and what is his missionary vision? To make these Gentiles into Jews? No. It is that Christ might be formed in them and this testimony of course is reflected in the response of the entire Church. Look at verse 23, **"They only heard the report: 'the man who formerly persecuted us is now preaching the faith that he once tried to destroy.' And they praised God because of me."**

Brothers and sisters, this land is calling out for testimonies that will authenticate the gospel of Jesus

Christ in such a way. The fact is that often the faith that we profess is just, let's face it, unbelievable . . . incredible. Thank God there have been these staggering beacons of light who have been a clear witness to the power and authenticity of the gospel of redeeming grace in the darkness of these past 30 years. Do you remember this story? Karen, a young girl, locking up the church hall after taking her Sunday school class. Life was good for her. She had just graduated from university and had got engaged. Her one great sadness was that her father had recently died. That night as she locked up a man walked up to her and said, "Karen", "Yes," she answered. "I've come for you," he said and pulled out a gun. "There must be some mistake," she said. "No mistake," he answered and fired. As Karen lay dying in her hospital bed, her mother weeping by her bedside, Karen said "I know you're broken hearted for me, Mum, but just think of the mothers of the boys who do such things. Think of how they must feel," and she gestured to her Bible and said, "Look, I want you to find one of these terrorists and give him my Bible and I want you to tell him that I love him". A week later Prison Fellowship had a meeting in Belfast. Chuck Colson was the keynote speaker. Before Colson was to speak, Liam McCluskey, a former member of the provisional IRA, a man who had been on dirty protest, a hunger striker, who became a follower of Christ, stood up, declared his faith in Christ and his renunciation of violence. Just as Colson was about to speak there was a security alert. A lady was walking up the aisle with her hand in a bag. A security guard rushed forward, but it was all right. She took her hand out of the bag and in it was a book. She went up to the platform and she embraced Liam McCluskey. "This week," she said, "I've lost a daughter, but tonight I've gained a son." Chuck Colson took the microphone and said to those who were assembled, "Nothing I could say to you could speak more powerfully than what you have just seen". That, brothers and sisters, is the self-authenticating power of the gospel. We need it desperately in this land.

Let's remember that Paul here is defending himself against the charge that he is not an apostle and that the gospel he preaches has not been sanctioned by 'mother Church'; his response is that he has received this from Jesus Christ, not from Jerusalem. His authority is in the gospel itself, not in the Church; and it is self-authenticating in the transformation of his life from a religious fanatic into an apostle of the Lord Jesus Christ. Well then, what is his relationship with the other apostles? How does he relate to the wider Church? This is what I want us to see as we come to the latter part of our study.

First, with regard to the synod, diocese, presbytery or congregation of Jerusalem (I am really trying to be sensitive to a wide ecclesiology) and then to the Church in Antioch. Why does he go to Jerusalem? I tell you he does *not* go because he is summoned to go. Remember Martin Luther – summoned to Leipzig. Paul was not summoned to Jerusalem; he went, he said, as a response to a revelation set before him. He went to Jerusalem because he was called by Christ to go there – not because he regarded Jerusalem as 'mother church'. For Paul, Jerusalem was not the mother church. Let us turn over to Galatians 4 verses 25 following now, as it is relevant to this. It is an obscure and difficult passage about Abraham's wife, Sarah, and her maidservant, Hagar. **"Now Hagar stands for Mount Sinai in Arabia and corresponds to the present city of Jerusalem,"** (the Jewish headquarters, which the Jewish Christians believed was the 'mother Church'), **"but,"** verse 25, **"but the Jerusalem that is above is free, and *she is our mother.*"** Do you see that? He is not answerable to Jerusalem on earth, but to the mother Church in Heaven where Christ Himself is exercising authority. When it comes to these apostles, Paul is willing to honour them, but he will not elevate them; in fact he is plain rude and cheeky about them. It's quite fun to read this! Look at chapter 2 verse 2. **"I went in response to a revelation and set before them the gospel that I preach among the Gentiles, but I did this privately to those who *seemed* to be leaders,"** – now these are the apostles in Jerusalem! And verse 6, **"As for those who *seemed* to be important . . ."** and verse 9, **"James, Peter and John, those *reputed* to be pillars in the Church."** What a cheeky chappie Paul is! You see he will honour them, but he will not elevate them or bow down to them the way these Judaisers are doing. Some of you may know Victor Griffin. Victor was, for many years, the Dean of St. Patrick's in Dublin. I suppose Victor could not be described as a classic evangelical but he was a great old school, low Church of Ireland man. I remember him saying at a function once, "Have you noticed," said Victor, "that those who dress up the most . . . seem to do the least?" He was of course referring to some of his colleagues in the Anglican Communion and he had little time for those who sought to elevate themselves in such a way.

So why does Paul go to Jerusalem? He tells us in chapter 2 verse 2, **"I went in response to a revelation and set before them the gospel that I preach among the Gentiles for fear that I was running or had run my race in vain."** It's not that Paul has any self-doubt about his vocation or calling. F.F. Bruce says this, "His commission was not derived from Jerusalem, but could not be executed effectively except in fellowship with Jerusalem. The gospel that he is preaching requires the support, the encouragement, the benediction of the entire church. Paul is a pioneer missionary but he is not a lone ranger." Evangelicals need to hear that, do they not? We are great at tactics, we produce all the spiritual entrepreneurs, but when it comes to strategy there are times when we are a total disaster. Imagine 'yours truly' arriving in Lucan almost 17 years ago. And when I arrived, I assumed Patrick had never come - never mind Columba and Columbanus; never mind all those who had been preaching the gospel in Lucan for generations before me. Let's assume my attitude was, 'Now I have come and I'm dreaming my dreams as to what is to take place in this area of God's vineyard'. That is how many of us think, and the fact that there happens to be a Christian 'McDonald's' serving marvellous

Big Macs, means that people at times are motivated to set up a sort of 'Burger King-dom' in order to offer spiritual whoppers next door, without any reference to what is going on in the whole Church Catholic. Now Paul will not think like this; he is functioning strategically, so he receives the blessing and the benediction of the entire Church in terms of his ministry of the gospel of grace to the Gentiles; and when he comes to establish rapport with them he uses outstanding relational skills which gives us an amazing insight as to how the Church is to function.

Most Church activities take place as a sort of cross between a courtroom and the annual general meeting of an insurance company. It's about as exciting as that. I remember my very first visit to a meeting of Presbytery. I sat beside this 'wag', who turned to me and said, "Don't worry about it, Trevor, the Catholics have purgatory and we have presbytery". In contrast, when it comes to Paul's activity with these apostles, the whole structure is fundamentally relational. It is not judicial. That's why he brings with him people like Barnabas and Titus who have these marvellous skills – personal, relational skills. One of them was a Jew, the other a Gentile. That's why Paul meets with them in private - so that they are not subject to all these lobbyists, who are trying to bring pressure to bear upon them. That is why, in his discussions, it is quite evident that he is flexible about everything - except the gospel. Wouldn't you love to be in church meetings like that, where everything is negotiable except the gospel? What was the result of this approach? Paul says, **"Nothing was added to the message . . . nothing."** They recognize that God is at work in different ways - Peter to the Jews, Paul to the Gentiles. It's what we would describe in the south of Ireland as horses for courses! Titus is accepted. He is a Gentile, but he is not compelled to be circumcised. The right hand of fellowship is also offered to Barnabas and Paul as fellow ministers of the gospel of Jesus Christ. The only thing that is requested of Paul and Barnabas is that they should **"remember the poor"**, which of course meant, "remember Jerusalem" - the poor despised, persecuted Christians of Jerusalem - and Paul never forgot them. Everywhere he went, he collected money to send to the poor of Jerusalem. Well, says Paul, the apostles are my allies and they share with me the same gospel.

It is clear that, in his approach to the church in Jerusalem, Paul's strategy is relational, but when it comes to the church in Antioch, and specifically to Peter, he is unquestionably confrontational. In Galatians chapter 2 verses 11 following, we have related one of the most tense and dramatic moments recorded in Holy Scripture. This is a head to head, eyeball to eyeball confrontation between two apostles. Peter, of course, is this wonderful man of God. You remember how the Spirit of God is poured out on him on the day of Pentecost and thousands of people respond as he stands and preaches the gospel. He has been given a special ministry to the Jews and specifically to Antioch because there are so many Jews there. The city had a population

of about half a million people of whom 65,000 were
Jews. What do we know of Peter? Well of course he is
a Christian. He confesses that Jesus is the Christ, the
Son of the living God. He believes the gospel as is clear
from verse 15; **"We who are Jews by birth and not
'Gentile sinners' know that a man is not justified by
observing the law, but by faith in Jesus Christ... So
we, too, have put our faith in Christ Jesus . . ."** And
Peter saw the implications of the gospel. He was willing
to live in fellowship with Gentiles without insisting that
they become Jews; to eat and drink with them; to sit
down at barbecues and have pork chops and spare ribs!
It was not a problem for him, but then something
happened. These visitors appear in Galatia, who have
obviously come to Antioch and they're putting pressure
on Peter not to eat with the Gentiles. The reason for
that, as we discovered yesterday, was that in the years
45 – 55 AD, leading up to the destruction of Jerusalem,
there was a resurgence of Jewish nationalism. There
was a real desire to rediscover the identity of Judaism
over and against the Romans, the Herodians and the
Samaritans, and for a passionate commitment to their
own people and for their ethos to be reborn. Now why
was Peter susceptible to this? Well, you see, Peter was
not just a Jew. Peter was a Jew from Galilee. He was a
Jew from a rural area of Galilee where Zealot activity
was rampant. It was where the paramilitaries had their
headquarters. Peter spoke with a thick Galilean accent
- that was how he was recognised in the courtyard. He
would have spoken with the equivalent of a sort of
Ballymena accent. People would have said, "Hey, weren't

you with this guy called Jesus?" Peter had received all the prejudices, attitudes, fears and suspicions about 'the other side' along with his mother's milk. It was deeply ingrained within him. So along come these characters, these passionate Jewish nationalists and they put pressure on Peter. Quietly they come to him and say, "Peter, you're a Jew, aren't you?" "Oh yes." "Aren't you proud to be a Jew, to be a son of Abraham?" "Yes," he said. "Well we want to accept you as one of our own. You don't want the poor Christians in Jerusalem to suffer, after all - do you, Peter?" "Oh no, I don't." "But if you continue as you are doing in terms of your ministry, in fellowship with these Gentiles, your mission to the Jews will be destroyed. They will not listen to you. You will be alienated from them." And Peter doesn't want to be misunderstood; he wants to be accepted; he wants to be effective as a missionary, as an apostle to the Jews - and he gives in.

You know this pressure, do you not? If you are a leader in the Church of Jesus Christ in Northern Ireland at this time, it's an enormous pressure. Let me be gentle with you and take you out of the Irish context altogether, to the southern states of America and the ministry of a man called John Perkins. We brought John over here a few years ago to speak at our own General Assembly. John is a black, Baptist preacher, who set up an amazing ministry in Mendenhall, Mississippi called 'the Voice of Calvary'. He saw clearly from the scriptures that the gospel of grace, the gospel of liberation not only affects us vertically, but that it affects us horizontally. It was an offence to the gospel that in the Mississippi Bible belt there was segregation between blacks and whites so that they could not worship together. Even when Billy Graham was invited to hold a crusade in Jackson, Mississippi the expectations were that as people came to faith in Christ the blacks would go back to their churches and the whites to their churches - utterly segregated. Perkins began an amazing ministry with the support of a number of others, two of whom were very close friends of his, both Presbyterian ministers in white churches. The social pressure, the peer pressure, on those two men to have nothing to do with the other side was such that eventually they both committed suicide. This is recorded in Perkins' book, 'Let Justice Roll Down'. Another American, Clarence Jordan, who is an adviser to Bill Clinton and a Christian man, paraphrases Galatians 2 verse 11 following in these terms, "But in spite of all this, when Rock (i.e. Peter) came to Albany (a city in East New York State), I had to rebuke him to his face because he was clearly in error. Before the committee appointed by Jim (i.e. James) arrived, he was eating with Negroes, but when they came he shrank back and segregated himself because he was afraid of the whites. He even got the rest of the white liberals to play the hypocrite with him so that even Barney (Barnabas) was carried away by their hypocrisy." Brothers and sisters, do you hear the power of this message for us in this country? I am chairman of a project of the Youth Board of the Presbyterian Church called 'Nexus Ireland'. It's a reconciliation project, which seeks to bring Catholic and Protestant young people together and lead them to such a radical commitment to Jesus Christ that every other loyalty and allegiance will become secondary. There was a time when we really struggled to find any young minister who would come on to the committee associated with Nexus Ireland. The reason they were giving (they were assistant ministers at the time) was that if they become identified with this, they would never, ever receive a call to a church. Well, this is *precisely* the pressure that was on Peter; it is exactly the same. The result of course is hypocrisy. People become unwilling to act on the basis of what they believe - unwilling to accept others on the basis that God accepts us. God recognizes that we are sinners, wretches without hope in the world, but he accepts us by faith alone in what He has accomplished for us upon the cross . . . but we are not willing to accept others on the same basis. This is hypocrisy. The reason why Paul is so adamant about this is, above all, because of its effect upon the gospel. He will not abandon the gospel of grace (the real thing) for a religion of obligation. What is the real thing? Well, here we come to it, and it is something in which I want you to revel.

To understand it you must grasp the concept of justification, the cry word of the Reformation. "This doctrine," says Martin Luther, "can never be taught and discussed enough. If it is lost and perishes then the whole knowledge of truth, life and salvation is lost and perishes at the same time. But if it flourishes everything good flourishes . . . religion, true worship, the glory of

God, and the right knowledge of all things and of all social conditions." We must rediscover the doctrine of justification by grace alone through faith alone. Here it is. What does 'justified' mean? I say it is the key word for the real thing because it appears over and over again. Look at verse 15, **"We who are Jews by birth and not 'Gentile sinners' know that a man is not justified by observing the law, but by faith in Jesus Christ. We, too, have put our faith in Christ Jesus that we may be justified by faith in Christ and not by observing the law, because by observing the law no-one will be justified."**

Let me adopt a definition of justification which has been used by Tom Wright, formerly the Dean of Lichfield; justification is simply to declare someone in the right. If you are justified, you are declared in the right. Some of you are familiar with a television programme called 'Rough Justice' in which hard cases are examined. They research court cases in which people have been unjustly imprisoned; they are in the right but they have been declared in the wrong. Many of them have suffered many, many years of incarceration before being liberated, set free and declared in the right as a result of the activity of politicians, lawyers and those in leadership on their behalf. These are people who are in the right although it is very difficult to have them declared in the right. How is it possible for those of us who are *in the wrong* to be declared *in the right*? That is the problem. We stand before God in His unimpeachable purity and holiness. We are answerable to him. We are unquestionably in the wrong. How can He declare us in the right? Now of course there are different answers given to this. The popular approach of the man in the street is to say, 'Well, you just need to be a decent person.' You probably realize that the man in the street has a theology, although he doesn't really know that he has. You hear it expressed now and again. The theology of the man in the street has three fundamental principles. The first of these is that good people go to heaven and bad people go to hell. The second is that the Lord helps those who help themselves; and the third principle is 'to err is human and to forgive is divine'. They place all of these elements together and operate on the basis that, if you do your best, . . . well, what else can God do but say it's going to be all right.

Now that is not the problem facing Paul in the church in Galatia. The problem in Galatia is bound up with those who are offering a religious approach as to how you can be declared in the right. They are arguing that somehow, by faith in Christ and by the works of the law, everything will be fine. Now that is a very common view in the church, Catholic and Protestant. On one occasion I was conducting a special series of evangelistic addresses in the convent school in Lucan. The subject for the evening was, 'If God is love, how can there be suffering?' When I had finished I thought that I had clearly presented the fact that God had taken our suffering upon Himself, that He had endured everything for us – even suffering the full force of His own anger in our place on the cross, so that all we have to do is to receive His salvation as a gift. Afterwards this dear woman came up to me and thanked me profusely. She said, "Thank you so much. That was marvellous, Trevor. It all goes to prove that we're going to have to try even harder". No, no, that's not it. *This is the real thing.* This is it - we are justified by faith alone in Christ alone. How can we be declared in the right if we are in the wrong? I hope that this won't confuse you, but the answer is that we are justified by works, but *not our works* . . . we are justified by the works of somebody else. You see, God does *not* say, "It's fine. It's O.K.. Everything is hunky dorey. I'll just smile at you on the Last Day." No. He has come Himself in Jesus Christ. He has lived perfectly for us; His righteousness is imputed to us; He bore our condemnation for us and He died in our place.

Before I studied theology I was a student at Magee College in Derry and in my first year I met this extraordinary man called T.S. Mooney. Some of you will know T.S. Mooney. 'T.S.', as he was known, was a bachelor and he used these memorable expressions like, "Women! The Lord bless them . . . and keep them!" He gave me a book by James Denny on 'The Death of Christ'. It is a wonderful book. In it James Denny writes, "The atonement of Christ, which is the basis of our justification, is summarized in these words,

> Bearing shame and scoffing rude, in my place condemned he stood;
> Sealed my pardon with his blood, Hallelujah! What a Saviour! "

If you are trusting in what Christ has done for you, you are justified. You are declared to be in the right, even though you are in the wrong. The real thing is simply 'amazing grace'.

Let us pray.

Lord, you know that whatever tradition we have come from in terms of our inheritance and background, it is so easy for us to become entangled in the works of the law. We say that we are saved by grace, but we have lived by law. Enable us today to enter into the liberation and joy of justifying grace. You have done everything, everything, everything for us. You accept us. We pray that as we meet others who are in Christ, whatever their politics, their nationality, their ethnicity, their gender, their religious inheritance or their tradition, that we may have grace to embrace them as brothers and sisters in Christ.

We ask this in Jesus' name, Amen.

"You told us we could drive through this stream!"
*"I just don't understand, because the water only comes
half way up the ducks!!"*

Faith not Work

Galatians 3

Some Americans had just arrived at Shannon airport, and they were looking forward to their sojourn through the Irish Republic. They hired a car and moved down through Clare to Kerry. As they came into a little village they noticed that there was a stream right through the middle of the main street. So they stopped the car and they turned to one of the residents and said to him, "Do you think it would be okay for us to drive through that stream?" And he said, "Oh, it'll be alright, O.K.. Drive straight through." So they got into the car and they began to drive, but when they got into the middle of the stream the car began to sink. Somehow they got the doors open and they swam to the bank. They turned to the Kerryman and said to him, "You told us we could drive through this stream!" "I just don't understand," he said, "because the water only comes half way up the ducks!!"

It's not just the Irish who are crazy. Listen to Eugene Peterson's marvellous paraphrase of this passage in 'The Message'. **"You crazy Galatians. Did someone give you an hallucinatory drug? Something crazy has happened. For it is obvious that you no longer have the crucified Christ in clear focus in your lives. He was certainly set before you clearly enough. Let me put this question**

to you. How did your new life begin? Was it by working your heads off to please God, or was it by responding to God's pleasure working in you? Are you going to continue this craziness? For only crazy people could think that they could complete by their own efforts what was begun by God. If you were not smart enough or strong enough to begin it, how in heaven's name do you suppose you could perfect it? Did you go through this whole painful process for nothing? You crazy Galatians!!"

The spotlight in Chapter 3 turns from the apostle Paul to the Galatians themselves. Do you remember 'Dad's Army'? Who could forget the pompous, disdainful, patronising Captain Mannering? The half-baked, 'Jones the butcher' – "Don't panic! Don't panic!" And Pikey, of course, who was as thick as champ. And Captain Mannering would turn disdainfully to Pikey and say, "You stupid boy." Well, here was Paul addressing his Christian brothers and sisters in Galatia in the same tone. I love J.B. Phillips' rather English translation, **"Oh, you dear, dear idiots!"** These are words of affection. Paul is perplexed; he is distraught by his brothers and sisters in Christ.

We know what is foolish. It is when we act in a way which is contrary to what we know, what we understand and what we have experienced. You know from childhood that fire burns, it is painful, it will cause discomfort to you, so to put your hand in the fire is an act of folly. You know to walk through certain parts of

Belfast or Dublin late at night is dangerous. You could be mugged or assaulted or worse; to do so is an act of sheer folly. As far as Paul is concerned these Christians in Galatia have gone crazy. They are foolish. They have begun to accept and embrace the teachings of these Judaisers - that faith in Jesus is not enough for our acceptance before God. Something else is required. **"This,"** says Paul, **"is foolishness. It is contrary to what you know, what you understand and what you have experienced. And the only possible reason for it is that you have been** (and here the translations vary) **bewitched, spellbound, charmed, beguiled."** Strong charismatic personalities have come into this fellowship . . . the sort who smile at you constantly. They look as if they have not only *seen* the Cheshire cat – but that they've *eaten* it. They would make, what we would call today, wonderful 'spin-doctors'. They have twisted the truth and seduced their minds.

Now young Christians are extremely vulnerable and the Christians in Galatia were young believers in Jesus Christ. Young Christians have certain needs - needs that are crying out to be satisfied. They want, and here we return to this theme again, they want a sense of identity. At one time these Galatians had been pagans, and they had known exactly who they were – they had had a clear sense of identity. At that time they would go off to the temples and they would offer their sacrifices. They would engage in sexual promiscuity with numerous priestesses who were called 'bees' - their responsibility was to collect the honey. These folk knew who they were. The Jews too knew who they were. But now they had come into a Christian community that recognised Jesus as the Saviour, the Messiah. Who are they now?

They were craving security. Any psychologist will tell you that a child brought up in a family where there are rules exercised in love will be happy and secure because they know what the limits are. A family without laws - without standards, where there is no good or bad, no right or wrong, where children are free to do whatever they like, where there is a sort of spiritual anarchy always results in unhappiness and insecurity for the children. Now this craving for security seems to have been met by the giving of the law, by conformity to the requirements of Judaism.

Of course, as young Christians, they want the blessing of God. They want to walk in the steps of God. They want to do what is right. That is why these agitators who have come into the church in Galatia are extremely attractive. They are saying to them, "Yes, it's great to believe in Jesus as the Messiah, as the Son of God, as the Saviour of the world . . . but if you were a part of our group, if you conformed to the ceremonies and rights of our community then you would know who you are. You are a Jew. You will feel the security of our fellowship with its lineage right back to Abraham. You will receive the blessing and benediction that the Lord has promised for His covenant people." Now let's face it, this is psychologically very, very attractive. This circumcision group are saying, "You have believed. Good. Now something else is needed."

I'm sure some of you are familiar with the activity of a group who call themselves the Church of Christ. I think they function in Belfast; they are quite strong in Dublin and they have a base in Lambeth in London. They basically target young Christian 'yuppies' - people who are relatively successful, who are middle-class. My daughter had an experience in Dublin. She was walking along past Trinity College when a very attractive girl came up to her and said "I am a Christian". And Ceri said, "Oh yes, I am a Christian too". "That's great," she said. "Would you like to come to my church?" And Ceri said, "Well yes, I would be quite happy to go to your church." So they entered into this conversation and my daughter, perhaps naively, handed over her name, address and telephone number. From that moment she was hounded by this girl on an almost a daily basis. You see, the philosophy of this group, who call themselves the Church of Christ, is that it is not enough for you to be a Christian in the sense that you believe in Jesus Christ; you must be part of their group. In fact you must be baptised by them, because they believe that it is only when you are baptised by them that you are regenerate.

Now we need to be careful here because it is possible for all of us to fall into this trap. I recognise that we come from many different denominational backgrounds with different confessional standards, which are important to us and so they should be. But I have discovered that it is vital in terms of mission in Lucan, where I function in West Dublin, that I establish no other criteria for fellowship in the Church of Jesus Christ than the standard that God establishes for our acceptance before Him - namely faith in Christ alone.

Historically there are two dangers for us in terms of the communities represented here on this island. There are those who are within the sacerdotal tradition who emphasise the sacraments. They will say that it is great to believe in Jesus as Christ, the Saviour of the world, but it is necessary for you to be incorporated into the sacramental life of our Church through rites and ceremonies performed by those who have been ordained by others who stand in apostolic succession. Now you will find that outlook both within the Roman Catholic and the Anglo-Catholic tradition. For me, according to the teaching of the apostle Paul in this context, this is adding to the Gospel.

Within the Reformed tradition there has emerged what Jim Packer calls 'orthodoxism'. That means that we are saying to people, "In order to accept you as brothers and sister in Jesus Christ it is not enough for you to profess faith in Him as Saviour and Lord. It is necessary for you to be able to articulate with clarity an orthodox doctrine of God, of Jesus and particularly of the means of your salvation." Imagine my situation in Lucan: if some people from a Roman Catholic background come and express faith in Jesus Christ, am I to say to them, "Well, it's great that you profess faith in Jesus Christ, but what is your doctrine of justification? Are you able to distinguish between the imputed righteousness of Jesus Christ and the imparted righteousness of Christ? What is your understanding of the Eucharist? What is your understanding of the real presence?" Am I supposed to go through a whole list of criteria before accepting them? Now we are not talking today about what is necessary as a confessional basis for a church; or about establishing relationships between different confessional communities. We are talking about the basis on which we accept another person as a brother or sister in Jesus Christ. If we expect, as sinful men and women, to be accepted before God on the basis of faith alone in Christ alone then we ought not to demand anything more from anyone else, no matter who they are or where they're from. That seems to be the clear teaching of this passage.

These Galatian Christians have been bewitched and beguiled into feeling that they have to become Jews in order to feel secure, to have an identity, to walk under the blessing of God. Paul tells them that this is foolishness for these three reasons:-

First, it is contrary to their understanding of the Gospel. Verse 1b **"Before your very eyes, Jesus Christ was clearly portrayed as crucified."** Literally the crucifixion was placarded as if it were a visual image. Now Paul is not saying that you constantly had before your ocular vision something like a stained glass window, an icon or a crucifix; what he is saying is that whatever you understood, you understood why Jesus Christ died for you. Intellectually and practically you grasped this basic fact. On the cross 'it is finished'. You have understood the significance of the crucifixion of Jesus Christ, that everything that had to be done, was done. So that anybody who says that you need to be circumcised, or that you need to eat only Kosher food, or that you need to have special Jewish festivals, or that ANYTHING ELSE is needed in order to be acceptable before God is denying the Gospel that you have understood. This is foolishness.

Second, it is contrary to your experience. At this point the apostle Paul bombards these Christians with a battery of questions concerning their experience of the Holy Spirit.

Verse 2 **"Did you receive the Spirit by observing the Law, or by believing what you heard?"**

Verse 3: **"Are you so foolish? After beginning with the Spirit, are you now trying to attain your goal by human effort?"**

Verse 5: **"Does God give you His Spirit and work miracles among you because you observe the law, or because you believe what you heard?"**

In terms of the experience of the Holy Spirit these Christians received the Spirit of God when they believed the Gospel - not through the observation of the Law, not by circumcision. Now the clear assumption here is that you cannot be a Christian unless you have the Holy Spirit. That is why we cannot talk about 'Christians' and 'born-again Christians'. Anyone who is born-again is a Christian because, **"If anyone does not have the Spirit of Christ, he does not belong to Christ." (Romans** 8 v.9) Now you have experienced and received the Holy Spirit through faith in the promises of God, not through the observation of the Law. **"Do you imagine,"** says the Apostle Paul, **"that having begun with the Holy Spirit you now can attain what God has purposed for you by your own efforts, merely by conformity to the law? Look,"** he says, **"when you are ministering in the Spirit - when the unction of God is upon you and signs and wonders are evident in miracle and healing - how does it take place? Through faith or observing the Law?"** Well, through faith. Always through faith.

I believe that all of us know something of what Paul is speaking of here. Most of us, including myself, have gone through arid and hard times where we have lived our lives in obedience to the law through obligation, carrying every conceivable yoke, except the yoke of Christ. Over 20 years ago I was appointed to be Moderator's assistant, that is I was appointed to look after a congregation when their minister became Moderator of the General Assembly. I was a young lad straight out of college. I was newly ordained. I'd never married anyone, never buried anyone, never celebrated communion, never baptised anyone and suddenly, overnight, I was responsible for about a thousand families. I was preaching two, sometimes three, times a week. I was burying two people a week. I was doing hospital visits. And, of course, because I found myself under this enormous obligation to conform to all the requirements of what a Presbyterian minister is meant to do - there was not a coffee morning organised by ladies that I did not bless with my presence. I reckoned that I was working some ninety to ninety-five hours a week. My marriage almost failed because of it. If Carys were here she would bear testimony to that. The reason was this - I was carrying a yoke in terms of obligation that was being imposed on me rather than the yoke of Jesus Christ. I remember one Sunday evening I came to that passage: **"Come to me all who are weary, and heavy laden and I will give you rest."** I stood before the congregation (in those days there were still some hats to be found). My opening line went something like this: "I have discovered this week that either Jesus Christ is a liar, or there is something desperately wrong with my life." Well, hats suddenly switched to the right; people sat bolt upright in amazement. You know what I'm talking about because, when we live in the Spirit, life is quite different. It may be demanding. We may even be suffering, but the yoke is easy and the burden is light. When we minister in the Spirit we find rest for our souls. Of course it is right to establish goals, to have a strategy, to know where we are going, but you know, individually and corporately, there is nothing like believing the promises of God and lifting up the sail and letting the wind blow. It is then that something happens. What the Galatians are doing is foolishness because it is contrary to their understanding of the Gospel and it is contrary to their experience of the Spirit.

Third, and this is the main emphasis of this passage - it is contrary to the Word of God. At this point in Paul's argument, Father Abraham appears on the stage. These Jews were so proud of their Father Abraham; they could trace their genealogical roots right back to him, and at a time of national conflict and identity crisis the Jewish people saw the answer, in Abraham, as to what it meant to be the people of God. He was not only the original source of blessing for the Jews but he was the Father of the Nation. They would have argued that Abraham was righteous, because of two things:- firstly, because he received the sign and seal of the covenant of grace, circumcision; and secondly, because of his obedience and faithfulness in keeping the Law, even before it was given to Moses. They reckoned that the ten trials that Abraham endured, culminating in his willingness to sacrifice Isaac, were paralleling the ten commandments. Therefore, they argued, those who do what Abraham did will be the righteous ones, because they have not only received the Law but because they keep the Law. "If that is your thesis," says Paul, "let's look at the text." He does this because the Judaisers were seeking to quote Scripture to show that faith was not enough. They argued that to be the true sons of Abraham you, like him, had to receive the sign and seal of the covenant in circumcision and to keep the commands of the Law. So at this point Paul turns to the Old Testament and asks, "What actually happens to Abraham in Ur of the

Chaldees?" What happens, says Paul, is that God meets with Abraham and makes him a promise.

To understand the nature of Paul's argument you must make this profound and essential theological distinction between law and promise. This is how you make the distinction: when you hear the words "I will," that's a promise. When you hear the words, "You will," that's the law. "I will," is a promise; "You will," is the Law. On the 28th of July, Carys and I celebrated our wedding anniversary. Let me take you back to the occasion twenty-eight years ago. Picture the scene as Carys and I stood facing one another in the church. Imagine that I had turned to her and said: "You will love me, you will honour me, you will obey me, you will stand by me whatever may come, you will make any adjustments to your life that are necessary so that you can genuinely share your life with me." Now if I had said that, what Carys would have said in response would have been unrepeatable. You see, marriage is not a contract, it is a covenant - a covenantal promise. I promised that I would love her, honour her and cherish her, that I would make any necessary adjustments in my life so that she could genuinely share her life with me and she reciprocated that. That is a promise. When God meets with Abraham, He makes the promise, **"I will . . . make of you a great Nation . . . so that your descendants are like the sands of the sea and the stars of the heavens . . . I will give you a land flowing with milk and honey. I will make you a blessing to the nations."** And Abraham believes the promise. And in this letter to the Galatians, Paul quotes from Genesis. **"It was credited - reckoned to him, for righteousness." (Galatians** 3 v.6 Genesis 15 v.6) So Abraham was declared in the right. How? Abraham hasn't a notion. He's no idea how God is accepting him, justifying him, declaring him righteous. But when he believes, it is so.

Here is what is important. Although Abraham was the Father of the Jews, he was justified when he was still a Gentile: he had not been circumcised. It was through faith that he was declared righteous. 'Now then,' says Paul, 'Who are the children of Abraham?' Not the Jews, per se; not those who can trace their genealogical descent from Abraham, but all who believe like Abraham . . . Jews and Gentiles alike. Verse 8: **"The Scriptures foresaw that God would justify the Gentiles by faith, and announced the Gospel in advance to Abraham: 'All nations will be blessed through you.' "** Now at this point, Paul goes back to the question; how then can we be justified before God? How can everything be alright, when everything is all wrong? How can we be declared in the right, when we are in the wrong? Paul says that there are two options. Option number one is, "Doing the law and living by it," Verse 12, and that's a quote from Leviticus 18. v.5. Alternatively, there is option number two which is the great watchword and cry of the Reformation, "Living by faith, because the just shall live by faith." Option number one means that you are a doer of the Law. Option number two means you're a believer in the promises.

Now if you go for option one, says Paul, which of course is the popular option today, just as it was in the days of the Apostle Paul – that is doing your best and seeking to conform to the requirements of the law - if you take that approach, you will be cursed, he says. This is strong language. When he mentions being cursed, he's not talking about voodoo, he's not talking about the evil eye. It is simply the opposite of blessing. Blessing is so important in the priestly and also in the prophetic ministry, when the priest would have raised his hands; or Aaron, having left the Holy of Holies, would raise his hand and bless the people; and that's why Jesus, exercising a priestly ministry, took the children into his arms and blessed them; and before he gave the Great Commission, He raised his hands and blessed his disciples. In blessing we are not praying. We are declaring the affirmation and acceptance of God. Cursing is the direct antithesis of this. It is the opposite of it, in which men and women are condemned. They are rejected. Now any of the Galatian Jews, reading what Paul has written here, would immediately turn their minds to the classic text in Deuteronomy, chapters 27 and 28, which would have been very familiar to them. It's an extraordinary picture of the Twelve Tribes of Israel depicted as an antiphonal choir. Six of them are on Mt. Gerizim; six are on Mt. Ebal. In the centre stand the Levites, who are reciting the litany of blessings for obedience and the catalogue of curses for disobedience. As they declare the litany of blessing for obedience the people scream, "Amen!" And as they recite the curses for disobedience the Tribes respond, "Amen!" Now Paul is speaking very bluntly here. He is saying that if you go for option one, if you choose to be justified by the works of the law, not only will you fail to receive the blessing of God and not be right with Him, much more seriously, you will receive the curse of God, the condemnation of God. The reason is that nobody can live by the law, no one. It is just not possible. All of us, Jews and Gentiles alike, disobey it because, **"There is none righteous, no not one." (Romans** 3 v.10). Tom Wright, whom I have quoted before, makes what I think is an amazing insight. He points out that the curses of Deuteronomy had already been fulfilled in the history of the Jewish people. Not merely in the lives of individual Jews, but Israel, as a whole, had failed in its mission to bring light to the nations. The entire history of Israel, from the Exodus to the Exile, was a commentary on the unleashing of the curses predicted in Deuteronomy; plagues, military defeat, national disgrace, anxiety, slavery and dispersion. One of the curses in Deuteronomy declares that, **"The Lord will bring a nation against you from far away, from the ends of the earth, like an eagle swooping down, a nation whose language you will not understand . . . they will devour the young of your livestock and the crops of your land until you are destroyed" (Deuteronomy** 28 v.49, 51) Tom Wright says, "Could any patriotic Jew of Paul's day walk through Jerusalem and see the Roman eagle ensconced near the temple precincts without thinking of that prophesy and its dire fulfilment? Therefore," he says, "in this passage Paul was reminding the Galatian agitators of something they should know, that the attempt to keep the Law, to do its works in Israel's history, had only led to failure and to the curse which the Law pronounces on those who fail to do it." **"Cursed are those who seek to be declared righteous by the works of the law."** That's option one.

Option two is our only hope. We cannot escape condemnation by our own works, but we can escape it by His. Verses 13 and 14: **"Christ redeemed us from the curse of the law by becoming a curse for us, for it is written: 'Cursed is everyone who is hung on a tree.' He redeemed us in order that the blessings given to Abraham might come to the Gentiles through Christ Jesus, so that by faith we might receive the promise of the Spirit."** Stephen Neil says that as the early church preached Jesus Christ and him crucified, "the Jewish listeners would have heckled by saying: 'Jesus is accursed!' " because they were familiar with this quotation from Deuteronomy. Now you know that the Jews did not practice crucifixion. The Talmud recognised four modes of capital punishment: stoning, burning, beheading and strangling. After the execution had been carried out, however, the corpse of the criminal would have been hoisted on to a piece of timber - a stake or a tree, as an indication that the person had been justly condemned as a transgressor of the divine law. Here is Paul's amazing declaration: **"Christ himself has redeemed us by enduring the curse of God for us."** He exposed himself to the curse of the law, that which we deserved. He Himself has embraced the curse, so that we, instead of receiving the curse, receive the blessing.

Whether Jew or Gentile, we receive it by faith. The consequence is that, by faith, the blessing to Abraham is for all, Jews and Gentiles alike.

Many people have said to me, "This is great, Trevor, but what about the law? Where does it fit in? Are you an antinomian?" That's a theological question. 'Anti' meaning against; 'nomos', meaning the law. There have been those, particularly in the 17th century among some of the Puritans, who were antinomian. They reckoned that the salvation of God was so exclusively of His grace that you could ignore the law. In fact the Law serves three purposes for Christian people.

Firstly, it is given to show us what sin is. To understand the purpose of the law in terms of Paul's argument you need to turn to Verse 25. I think that this is the key verse for understanding the nature of the law. **"Now that faith has come, we are no longer under the supervision of the law."** The word for 'supervision' in the Greek is 'paidagogos' from which we have the word 'paedagogue', a disciplinarian. If you were a person of some importance and wealth, living in the Greco-Roman world, you would have appointed two people to help educate your children. You would have appointed a tutor, a teacher to instruct them in the values and philosophy that was close to your heart; but you would also appoint a paedagogue, a supervisor to discipline your children and keep them in order. As a result most of the images that we have concerning paedagogues depicts them with either a cane or a rod. The word 'paedagogue' conveys the impression of something essentially negative -not completely, but essentially. What then is the supervisory role of the law?   How does the paedagogue function? Verse 19: **"What then was the purpose of the Law? It was added because of transgressions until the Seed to whom the promise referred had come."** What Paul is saying is that there was sin before the law came, but, in order for us to understand the nature of our sin, the law has been given. It's rather like driving in Dublin. You know there are only two types of driver in Dublin; the quick and the dead. We have to warn tourists consistently, particularly Americans, that they must not stop when the traffic lights turn to red . . . at least not immediately, because if they do two cars will ram them from behind. Someone told me recently of a plan to move the traffic from the left hand side of the road to the right hand side, because of the Europeanising of the Irish Republic and the benefits which we have received because of our incorporation into the EU. What they plan to do is to move all the trucks over on the Monday, and if it's successful, they'll move the cars over on the Tuesday, and if you drive in Dublin you will realise that people will notice no difference whatsoever! Now, in order to avoid accidents traffic laws are established so that we will know what is acceptable and what is unacceptable. And the Law has been given in order for us to know what sin is. It provides the standard. It reveals the character of God, the nature of God, the moral requirements of God.

Secondly, Verses 19 and 20; **"The law was given through**

intermediaries, Moses and the Angels, and therefore does not provide direct access to God." Now that is a difficult concept for us to grasp. Paul is assuming that angels were present when Moses received the law of God at Mt. Sinai. That is not specifically recorded anywhere in the Scriptures, but the presence of angels always indicated that God was revealing himself. You remember Jacob lying on the stone and he sees this ladder rising to heaven and on it, ascending and descending are angels, and God comes and stands beside Jacob. Similarly at the birth of Jesus Christ there are angels everywhere, aren't there? The angel Gabriel comes and speaks to Mary, then he brings a message to Joseph and then, the multitude of the Heavenly Host appear, praising God. There are angels because God himself has come incarnate. So it is assumed that, at Mt. Sinai, these angels have come with Moses in order to communicate the Torah, the law. However, since the law has been communicated through intermediaries, it means that through the law we do not have direct access to God. If we are dependent only on the law we will not have spiritual life - only God Himself can give life. Now this is really important to us, because I have attended places of worship, as you have, that seem to be meticulously conformed to the requirements of the law which has been handed to us, if you like, through intermediaries. We had a young curate priest in Lucan who was quite a character. If you're from a Catholic background you will realise that the quicker you can say mass, the bigger the crowd you will get. This priest could do the whole works - prayers, homily, eucharist, offering, all in thirty-two minutes flat. I remember standing beside him on one occasion as he said the Lord's prayer. I thought he was speaking in tongues. There was a spiritual emptiness, you see. I have been at services in totally reformed, orthodox, evangelical congregations, some of which, I have to confess, that I was conducting myself. I remember thinking to myself that if I wasn't being paid to do this I wouldn't be here at all. It was so grim. Everything was meticulously correct, but there was no spiritual vibrancy. There was no life. Listen to these wonderful words of Eugene Peterson: "The word 'Christian' means different things to different people. To one person it means a stiff, uptight, inflexible way of life, colourless and unbending. To another it means a risky surprise-filled venture, lived tip-toe at the edge of expectation." Both of these pictures can be supported with evidence. There are innumerable examples for each situation in congregations all over the world. However, if we restrict ourselves to biblical evidence, only the second image can be supported, that is the image of the person living zestfully, exploring every experience - pain and joy, enigma and insight, fulfilment and frustration - as a dimension of human freedom and searching through each for sense and grace. If we get our information from the biblical material, there can be no doubt that the Christian life is a dancing, leaping, daring life. The law cannot produce this, because it comes through intermediaries. Only God Himself can produce this.

Thirdly, the law shows us that we are prisoners (Verses

22 and 23). In the words of Malcolm Muggeridge, "We are trapped in the dark little dungeons of our own egos." That's what the law does to us. As we see its standards, its requirements and its obligations, it highlights and underlines just how wretched we are. I am astounded that people say to me, "I live by the ten Commandments . . . I follow the sermon on the Mount." "Good for you," I say. I have been a Christian, practically all my life, but the older I get and the more I understand the nature of the holiness and righteousness of God, the more I want to sing hymns like,

> Just and holy is Thy Name,
> I am all unrighteousness,
> Vile and full of sin I am
> Thou art full of truth and grace.

Brothers and Sisters that's what the law does to us. No wonder Paul says that, when we understand the role of the law, it just drives us to Jesus Christ. He is our only hope because He himself has endured for us the curse and condemnation that we deserve.

Finally, how does the law fit into the purposes of God? Now I'm going to use a brief analogy. It comes from Dick Lucas, who recently retired from St. Helen's, Bishopsgate in London. He depicts a newly-born child. That young child is full of promise and we come to it with all sorts of dreams and hopes. We pour our energies and creativity into that child, but when self-consciousness comes the law is required. So to the little child you say, "You will not pull the cat's tail; you will not pour milk over your sister's head." And perhaps more importantly, "You will not lie or steal." You are establishing a law. This is the standard, but when the child reaches maturity, when they leave the nest, the law is no longer external, but hopefully, that child will have imbibed the values which you have communicated to it. The whole value system becomes internalised. The outcome is that when my son is walking through Trinity College, Dublin, where he studies, he does not have in front of him these external requirements. No, they have become part and parcel of his life. When you throw yourself upon Jesus Christ and embrace him as Lord and Saviour, the Spirit, apart from whom you cannot be a Christian, comes within you so that the law which was external is now written in your heart. That's why Paul says that we are no longer under the paedagogue, the external supervision of the law. Those who believe, have the Spirit of Christ within them. The law is now on their hearts. You are no longer under the external supervision of the law; you are now under the internal discipline and tutelage of Christ.

How then do you live? Well, if there is one verse which summarizes almost everything that Paul wants to say in his letter to the Galatians, I think it is Chapter 5, verse 6. Remember this verse if you forget everything else. This is how we are to live.

" The only thing that counts is faith expressing itself in love."

"We're in a fine pickle now. We don't know where we
are, and he doesn't know who he is."

Sons not Slaves

Galatians 3 v.26 – 4 v.31

A number of British soldiers got lost in the Arabian desert during the Gulf War. They were from the Royal Irish Regiment and as they were staggering through the desert they were confronted by a 5 star American general. They said to him, "Do you know where we are?" The general was outraged that they had not saluted him, that they were unkempt in their appearance, that they were not speaking to him directly and that they did not address him as "Sir". He said to them, "Do you know who I am?" And the young private turned to his mate and said, "We're in a fine pickle now. We don't know where we are, and he doesn't know who he is."

Who am I? That is the great question of identity isn't it? Well, I am the son of Robert and May; I'm the brother of Merrill; I'm the husband of Carys who is Welsh, the father to Peter who is Canadian - Ceri my daughter is Irish, but mercifully we all speak English. I'm an Irishman from Ulster of Scottish descent; I am Catholic, Evangelical and Reformed; I am a Presbyterian minister in Lucan, west of Dublin, when I am not skiing. That's some insight into who I am.

Identity is the major issue facing the Jews who have arrived in Galatia from Jerusalem. They want to respond

to the question, "Who am I?" with the answer, "I am a
Jew." Now they mean by that their ethnic, national
and religious identity - that they were God's people,
the true descendents of Abraham, a people who had
been promised a piece of land that would stretch from
Dan to Beersheba. The nationalism that they expressed
is an ethnic nationalism. You remember that we
distinguished between civil nationalism and ethnic
nationalism? Civil nationalism says everybody who was
born here and who lives here belongs here. Ethnic
nationalism says everybody who is the same as us in
terms of race and religion belongs here. Of course these
Galatian Jews knew who they were; they knew who they
were because they kept the law. They were committed
to circumcision, to the eating of kosher food and to
special holy days. They recognised that the Gentiles
could become part of this provided that they became
like them. So these Christian Jews who had come down
from Jerusalem in order to preserve their identity at a
time of resurgent nationalism were saying, "Yes, we
believe Jesus is the Christ, the Son of God, the Saviour
of the world . . . but Gentiles must become Jews, they
must keep the law in order to be right with God." Paul
is refuting all of this; he will have none of it. Firstly he
says, "Abraham was given a promise and believed in
God while he was still a Gentile; in addition he was
declared in the right with God without the law".
Secondly, the law was given as the standard of God to
show us our sin and our need of a saviour. Thirdly, it is
Jesus Christ alone who causes us to be declared in the
right and who is received by faith alone.

Paul now comes to the climax of his thesis. Let me explain, for a moment, how a Rabbi functions in terms of argument. Most of us, the inheritors of Graeco-Roman thought forms, begin with a premise and work to our conclusion, so that we say what we really want to say, we draw upon all our arguments and our primary thesis comes at the end. Now throughout the Scriptures, there is a rabbinic form of communication and argument known as the principle of inversion and it is enormously helpful to know this when you are reading the Scriptures, especially the prophets and the Psalms. Certainly the apostle Paul argues like this. You find that he will present argument one, argument two and argument three; then he reaches the main thrust of his thesis, but then he will argue number three, number two and number one. That's the principle of inversion. This happens over and over again and you find it, for example, in Isaiah 53 and in Paul's letter to the Corinthians. We find him doing the same thing here in Galatians; he has argued one, two and three. Now this is the climax, this is the fulcrum, this is the pinnacle, this is the vista from which he wants us to see the primary thrust of his message. Galatians, ch.3 v. 26. Here it is:- **"You are all sons of God through faith in Christ Jesus."**

You are all sons of God through faith in Christ Jesus. *This* is our primary identity. We are members of the family of God and, as the sons of God, we are the inheritors of all that the Father has promised to us. Now, says Paul, this is not possible through the keeping of the law but only through faith in Jesus Christ. He turns to these Christians in Galatia and says, "Do you remember what happened at your baptism? When you were baptised, you were baptised into Christ." Now when I hear that my mind turns immediately back to the argument and debate that was going on in the church in Corinth. Whether you realize it or not, the conflict in Corinth was also over ethnicity, over different social, nationalistic and ethnic groups. Those who claimed to be the followers of Paul were Romans - 'Paul' is a Roman name; those who were followers of 'Apollos' were Greeks - that's a Greek name; those who were the followers of 'Peter' claimed to be the followers of 'Cephas' - they were Aramaic speaking Jews, and Cephas is the Aramaic term for Peter. There were those, of course, who claimed to be non denominational Christians and said that they were just followers of Jesus Christ. The church in Corinth is divided into these various ethnic groupings. "Now," says Paul to the church in Corinth, "Who were you baptised into? You were not baptised into Paul; you were not baptised a Roman or a Greek or a Jew. You were baptised into Jesus Christ." And here he is saying to the Christians in Galatia, "You were not baptised into Abraham." It was not a *tribal* initiation ceremony. I do think we need to hear that in this country do we not? We are brought in baptism into union with Christ and therefore with all who are in Him. This is your family; you are the sons of God through the Son of God. When you were baptised into Christ, Paul says, "Did you not put on Christ?" Everything which He has inherited as a Son is yours and everything that He has been given is now yours.

What we're speaking about here is an exclusive identity. Sonship is only possible for those who are in union with God through faith in Jesus Christ. It is an exclusive identity - but now, Paul says, it is an all-embracing identity. Think of those elements which cause the most conflict and division within the world. What are the sources of fundamental human cleavage? There is ethnicity. Think of the wars that have taken place throughout the world, even throughout this century; the conflicts between Hutu and Tutsi, between Serbs and Kosovars, between Celts and Anglo Saxons, between Unionists and Nationalists, between Jews and Gentiles. There is the cleavage of ethnicity and there is the conflict concerning economics; in places like India, of course, there is the social and economic distinction between the upper caste and the lower caste; in Britain and in Ireland, between the middle class and the working class; in the world, between those who have and those who have not. In Paul's day there was the conflict between slave and free, and in our day there is the great tension expressed in the gender wars between men and women as to their role, their status and their position. At this point, I believe, Paul becomes his most magisterial. Confronted with these primary elements that divide us of race, money and sex, he makes this extraordinary declaration. The sons of God, Jew and Gentile, bond and free, male and female **"are all one in Jesus Christ."** (Galatians 3 v.28) This is an extraordinary statement; we are all equal and it is a radical equality for the sons of God. There are few statements in Scripture that are more applicable to the context in which we live than this.

The Church in Ireland over the past centuries has
reflected the brokeness and divisions of the world. Even
the denominations that we have inherited, of which
many of us are members, reflect such ethnic divisions.
The Church of Ireland from England, the Presbyterians
from Scotland, and the Roman Catholics of Celtic Ireland.
It is one reason why I am convinced that the Reformation
never really took hold in Ireland. The doctrines of grace
have never really been heard in Celtic Ireland because
they are so closely interwoven with nationality and
ethnicity. Evangelicals particularly, have so elevated,
honoured and embraced middle class values and ideals
that those from working class backgrounds struggle to
be assimilated into the fellowship of our churches. In
the past, God forgive us, we had to set up ministries -
wonderful ministries like the Belfast City Mission -
because poor people did not have the appropriate clothes
to wear to worship in the churches with those who
claimed to honour and serve the living God. And our
evangelicalism in this country is appallingly patriarchal
and chauvinistic. Just listen to the male humour. It is
consistently a put-down of women. The radical equality
that Paul indicates for Sonship in the terms of the
Kingdom of God means that today women are patronised
by being asked only to make tea, to knit blankets and
to arrange flowers. There is something staggeringly
liberating in this declaration of the apostle Paul that,
as the sons of God, Jew and Greek, male and female,
bond and free are one - they are equal.

Now let me make a point that I think is a corollary of

this; because they are equal it does not mean that they are the same. Paul does not cease to be a man and he does not cease to be a free man (it is such an asset for him in terms of his missionary endeavours - that is why he ends up in Rome) and he never ceases to be a Jew. That is why, when he is describing his strategy for mission, he says, **"I became all things to all men to win some."** He says, **"To the Jews I became a Jew."** He does not say, "To the Gentiles, I became a Gentile", he says, **"To the weak I became weak"** because he cannot become a Gentile. Why? Because he is a Jew. Do you see the implications of what I am saying? If you're a man you remain a man; if you're a business man you remain a business man; if you're a unionist and British you remain a unionist and British because that is who you are. You do not cease to be who you are, but if you are a son of God you are equal with those in Christ who are different from you, women, workers, republicans, nationalists. Do you see the extraordinary implications of this statement for the country in which we live? If men and women who honour Jesus Christ as Saviour and Lord embraced their brothers and sisters, whatever their political view, whatever their gender, whatever their social and economic standing, it would be revolutionary in terms of a peace process.

Paul says you have a choice - to be a son or a slave. In Galatians 4 v.8 you will see what you were like before you were Christian. **"Formerly, when you did not know God, you were slaves to those who by nature are not gods. But now that you know God - or rather are known**

by God - how is it that you are turning back to those weak and miserable principles?" Now before they became Christians, Paul says they didn't know God. Of course they had an awareness of God, (self consciousness produces God consciousness), but the language of knowledge here is the same language of intimacy which is used when we read that Adam 'knew' his wife. They did not know God, nor were they known by God in this sense; instead they were trapped by weak and miserable principles. Now we don't have time to give a seminar on the elemental principles of the universe that were predominant in the world of Galatia and were rampant in Celtic Ireland before the arrival of Patrick and the preaching of the gospel. But essentially these elemental principles are divided into two: there were the earthy ones, earth, fire, air and water, and there were the heavenly ones, the sun, the moon and the stars. It was believed that all of these elements functioned together with us holistically, so that what took place was inevitable, "que sera, sera, whatever will be, will be." We were driven by fate. Now of course you can see this in contemporary movies. I referred the other morning to "Star Wars: Episode 1" – "Don't think, feel; and may the force go with you," as they seek for the one that fate had determined for them. You see it in a movie like 'The Lion King', and not least in Elton John's title song, 'The Circle of Life'. In such a view, all of reality functions in a cyclical fashion; all of the elements that constitute the universe are interacting with one another and repeating themselves over and over and over again. This is unlike a Judeo-Christian understanding of life which has a creation and a consummation. There is an end in terms of the coming of the Lord Jesus Christ. Now all of this has had a profound effect upon us even today. You and I know the great appeal of astrology. Most of us sitting in the waiting room at the dentist's or at the doctor's have had a little glance on the basis of our star sign to see what is in store for us, have we not? And there is still an element of superstition, particularly in Ireland, about walking under ladders or being confronted by black cats. If you happen to come from county Tyrone, you know that it's a sure sign of a death in the family if there's a frog in the house. Well I <u>do</u> hope that as Christians you walk under ladders . . . <u>and</u> play with black cats and invite frogs into your home! These are weak and miserable principles, says Paul; they don't work, they lead to slavery and the marks of such slavery are of course techniques which have to be performed, laws that have to be observed and days that you have to remember. The result is that today you find people engaging in all forms of weird and wonderful meditation, holding hands and humming or repeating weird mantras like, 'Listen to the sound of one hand clapping'. Well of course this is gibberish, it's gobbledygook.

A few years ago I was ill after I had returned from Thailand. I had a strange condition caused by parasites in my intestine. It was pretty awful. A lady, who I know quite well in Lucan, who's a wonderful artist, came up to me one day and said, "I hear you're unwell," and she held onto my hands very tightly and started rubbing the back of my right hand. Then she said, "At 12 o'clock tomorrow I want you to turn on all the water in your house; I will open all the taps in my house and it will flush it out of your system." Here we have the same phenomenon in Galatia. These people reckoned that if they observed all these rules and regulations, special days, times of prayer and pilgrimages, then they would be on track with God. In fact, says Paul, the result is slavery as people are driven and controlled by the elemental principles of the universe. It is, he said, a life of slavery.

Now some people have tried to suggest that the apostle Paul is arguing here that Judaism is pagan. I think not. Turn back to Galatians chapter 4 verse one: **"What I am saying is that as long as the heir is a child, he is no different from a slave, although he owns the whole estate. He is subject to guardians and trustees until the time set by his father. So also, when we were children, we were in slavery under the basic principles of the universe."**   The Jews were the heirs of the promises of God. They were so privileged, weren't they? They had received not only the promise, but also the law of God. It functioned, as we discovered yesterday, as a paedagogue . . . as a supervisor. The law was good - it revealed the character, the standards of God - but the law, says Paul, came under demonic influence under the principles of this world. Satan exploited the law to make us slaves, so that what was good was distorted. Now the Jews believed that it was necessary to keep these laws in order to have what you want, in order that your needs might be satisfied. What Paul is saying here is simply this; Jewish practice, apart from faith in the promises of God, is slavery, and let me say quite clearly that Christian practice, apart from faith in the promises of God, is also slavery.

The two branches of Christendom which are most prominent in this country are, what Michael Cassidy calls, the 'high and hazy' and the 'low and lazy'. The high and hazy, of course, are those who are sacerdotal, those who major on the sacraments. Thus, within the Roman Catholic and Anglo Catholic tradition, you are received sacramentally into the life of the Church and you are encouraged to participate in the life of the Church and through obedience to the laws that are laid before you, you are expected to develop a life of righteousness. In the evangelical tradition, the low and lazy, we hope self righteously, that we are better than that. Well, what happens, in fact, is that evangelical people simply have a different sacramental rite; you raise your hand, you come to the front, you sign a decision card and perhaps you go through some ceremony. So now that you are in the Kingdom of God, what happens to you? You are handed a list of rules and you are told that if you conform to those rules and regulations - if you comply with all that is laid before you in terms of obligation – then you are on the path of righteousness. In my opinion, this is the Christian faith *apart from* faith in the promises of God. It is slavery. Ministers in many Christian churches stand before their people every Sunday beating them, whipping them and hammering them with the law. In fact they assess the value and virtue of a service of worship by judging how miserable you feel afterwards! I was preaching in Hamilton Road in Bangor many years ago and I must have been engaged in this form of activity. Afterwards a woman met me at the door and she shook my hand and said, "That was a great service Mr. Morrow. I feel really terrible." One man said to me recently, "My minister does not realise that a Good Friday Agreement was signed 2,000 years ago. Every Sunday morning he engages in paramilitary beatings." This is pure slavery; and how do you know if you are a slave? When you estimate your worth exclusively on the basis of what you do and how you perform. A slave has no other purpose; he has no other value, but to conform to the duties and obligations that are laid before him.

Now, says Paul, in order to set us free from all of this, God has done two things. Firstly, He has sent His Son (Galatians 4 verse 4); and secondly, He has sent His Holy Spirit (Galatians 4 verses 6 and 7). In order that we might not only live like sons but be given the full legal status of adopted sons, God has done something for us in his son Jesus Christ. It was quite common in Roman law for adoption to be practised. In fact several emperors adopted men, who were not related to them, in order to give them their office and authority. An adopted son was, in all legal respects, equal with those born into the family. They were given the same name, the same inheritance, the same position and the same rights as the natural born son. Now, says Paul, God sent his Son, who by his divine nature was the son of God, in order that we who are not his children by nature might be his children by adoption and thus receive the full rights of sons. Do you realise that we have the same name, the same inheritance, the same position, the same rights as the very Son of God by virtue of His divine nature? That is who we are. Extraordinary! We are the sons of the living God; how has He achieved this? It was by an amazing act of redemption, to set us free from slavery.

In the Graeco-Roman world a man of wealth was free to choose to liberate a slave out of compassion or affection or as an act of justice. This is what he would do. He would go to the temple or shrine and he would deposit a sum of money, the required amount to liberate a slave. Once the redemption price had been paid to the recent owner the slave was redeemed. He can never, never again be enslaved. This is what God has done. He sent His Son born of a woman, as we were, under the law, which He kept perfectly as a man because the law is holy and just and good. He came to redeem those under the law and, because we are all cursed, so He was cursed for us. Listen to what James Denny writes in his book 'The Death of Christ':– "Christ not only became man bound to obedience, but He became cursed for us. He made our doom His own; He took on Himself, not only the calling of a man, but the responsibility of sinful men. It is in this, that His work as our Redeemer lies, for it is in this that the measure - or rather the immensity of His love is seen." Through the cross we have been redeemed, we are adopted sons, valuable - not because of what we do - but because of who we are.

I love the story of Billy Bray, the 18th century miner, who was gloriously converted to Jesus Christ through the reading of John Bunyan's Pilgrims Progress and went on to become a Methodist lay preacher. He started out as a rather rough-hewn, foul-mouthed miner and came to faith in Jesus Christ sitting in a rather sedate Anglican church in Truro, when the reality of this truth dawned upon his soul. He stood up and began clambering over the pews to the amazement to everyone around him, shouting, "I'm the son of a king! I'm the son of a king!" And why wouldn't he shout ?! – That's who we are, a people redeemed from slavery and given the full rights of adopted sons. God has sent his Son, and secondly, He has sent His Spirit so that His Spirit might witness with our spirits to assure us that we are the sons of God and enable us to cry out with the intimacy of a little child, "Abba, Father." Thomas Goodwin the puritan, has this lovely illustration. He says that, when the Spirit does this, it's rather like when you're walking along with your little son by the hand. He knows that he's your son, but, for no real reason except that you just love him, you reach down and you lift him up and you hug him. Goodwin says that it is like this when love is poured into our hearts by the Holy Spirit and we know, we know of a certainty that we are the sons of God

Let me say something quite sombre; some of you are slaves, not sons, and some of you are sons but you are living like slaves. I say some of you are slaves and not sons. I don't care what your theological convictions are. I don't care what tradition you come from. Jack Miller was Professor of Evangelism and Apologetics at Westminster Theological Seminary when I was a student there. Jack said to me, "Do you know what's so amazing. We can bring students into a totally orthodox reformed seminary, who have been brought up in the niceties of reformed orthodoxy, but they are slaves; they are not regenerate; they are not born of God." Of course, that was the experience of John Wesley, was it not? This is how John Stott describes it, "Wesley in his post-graduate Oxford days was in the Holy Club. He was the son of a clergyman and already a clergyman himself. He was orthodox in belief, religious in practice, upright in conduct and full of good works. He and his friends visited the inmates of the prisons and workhouses in Oxford; they took pity on the slum children of the city providing them with food, clothing and education; they observed Saturday as the Sabbath as well as Sunday; they went to church and to holy communion, they gave alms, they searched the Scriptures, they fasted and prayed, but they were bound in the fetters of their own religion for they were trusting in themselves that they were righteous instead of putting their trust in Jesus Christ and Him crucified." Well, you know what happened to John Wesley in Aldersgate Street? He felt his heart strangely warmed and he said, "I put my trust in Christ, in Christ alone for salvation and I was given an inward assurance that my sins, even my sins, had been taken away." Now here is

Wesley looking back at this, writing in his journal and he says this, "I had, even then, the faith of a slave though not that of a son."

Some of you are slaves and not sons, and some of you are sons but you live like slaves. There is no freedom, there is no fervour and there is no sense of God's favour. If I may quote Jack Miller again, "You say the words of grace but you cannot sing the melody." The thundering voice of the apostle Paul comes to you this morning, "What has happened to all your joy?"

I think you realise by now that I am quite a mischievous character. We always have a chuckle sometime during morning worship in Lucan, not I think for affected reasons, but simply because that's who we are. It's an expression of our humanity and we need these experiences do we not? I found this lovely story by Chuck Swindoll. He was preaching at a conference and a woman came and handed him a note. It said, "Humour has done a lot to me in my spiritual life. How could I have reared twelve children, starting at age 32, and not have had a sense of humour? After your talk last night I was enjoying some relaxed moments with friends whom I met here. I told them I got married at age 31. I didn't worry about getting married because I left my future in God's hands. But I must tell you that every night I hung a pair of men's trousers on my bed and knelt down to pray this prayer,

> "Father in Heaven hear my prayer and grant it if you can,

I've hung a pair of trousers here, please fill them with a man."

Swindoll says that the following Sunday he read that humorous letter to his congregation. They enjoyed it immensely, but he happened to notice the different reactions of a father and his teenage son. The Dad laughed out loud, but the son seemed preoccupied. On that particular Sunday the mother of this family had stayed at home with her sick daughter. Obviously neither father nor son mentioned the story because a couple of weeks later Swindoll received a note from the mother. "Dear Chuck, I'm wondering if I should be worried about something. It has to do with our son. For the last two weeks I have noticed that before our son turns the light out and goes to sleep at night, he hangs a woman's bikini over the foot of his bed." It's great to be a Christian! It is the most wonderful thing in the world. To the people of Northern Ireland we have to say, "What has happened to all your joy?" What has happened to evangelical Christendom in Ulster is what happened to these saints in Galatia. They have grown hard and cynical and critical and censorious and judgmental. Ulster evangelicalism is full of this spirit and Paul is bold enough to give us the reasons why. There are three reasons for their joyless enslavement.

Firstly, in terms of the community they had become sectarian. Look at verse 17, **"Those people are zealous to win you over, but for no good. What they want is to alienate you from us so that you may be zealous**

for them." What these characters are concerned about is creating a community that can clearly delineate and set "us" apart from "them": Paul over there, us over here - have nothing to do with him. If you have anything to do with him, you can't have anything to do with us. Do you recognise this? Joe Liechty is a very close personal friend of mine. He's a member of my congregation in Lucan and also a member of 'my small group'. Joe is probably a world expert on sectarianism. He's been researching in Ireland on this subject for many years and this is his definition:– "Sectarianism is a complex of attitudes, beliefs, behaviours and structures in which religion is a significant component and which influences or causes destructive conflict by :- (1.) belittling or demonising rival groups, (2.) reinforcing the boundaries between rival groups or (3) justifying or enabling the domination of rival groups." This is what we have here; a community that has become sectarian.

Secondly, an understanding of mission that focuses on proselytism. Do you know that expression? The purpose of proselytism is to make other people the same as us. Look again at verse 17. **"Those people are zealous to win you over but for no good. What they want is to alienate you from us so that you may be zealous for them."** They want to make sure that you're part of their group and that you have developed a pattern, a lifestyle, an attitude where your primary intent in terms of mission is to make other people followers, not of Christ, but of them. This is so different from the apostle

Paul's vision that Christ might be formed in them. This vision was that they might be the same as these Jews. I notice that in terms of my ministry. When I come north and bear witness to what we are doing in Lucan, people will say to me, "Have you got lots of converted Roman Catholics?" What do they mean by that? What they mean is, "Have I got people who are no longer Roman Catholics but the same as us?" Well, I want to tell you that that is not what my ministry is about. My commitment is to bring people under the lordship of Jesus Christ regardless of what tradition they come from. The missionary strategy which we find in Galatia is one of proselytizing.

Thirdly, there is legalism. We know about that, of course, from the whole structure of Paul's argument. Legalism is so destructive isn't it? Lewis Johnson was a professor in Dallas Theological Seminary and he spent a year with me at Edinburgh University from 1974-75 and he wrote this, "One of the most serious problems facing the orthodox Christian Church today is the problem of legalism. One of the most serious problems facing the Church in Paul's day was the problem of legalism. In every day it is the same. Legalism wrenches the joy of the Lord from a Christian believer and with the joy of the Lord goes his power for vital worship and vibrant service. Nothing is left but cramped, sombre, dull and listless profession. The truth is betrayed and the glorious name of the Lord becomes a synonym for a gloomy kill-joy. The Christian under law is a miserable parody of the real thing." Here is joyless slavery that is rampant throughout this land, the land of which Steve Stockman calls "The Land of the '*Thou shalt nots*' " in his poem of the same title.

> "Thou shalt not swear, thou shalt not drink,
> thou shalt not joke, thou shalt not think,
> Thou shalt not hear, thou shalt not see,
> thou shalt not say, thou shalt not be,
> Thou shalt settle down in the trenches
> in the land of the '*thou shalt nots*'.
> What on earth then can you do then?
> My goodness I forgot.
> Thou shalt go to church on Sunday,
> thou shalt wear a plastic smile,
> Thou shalt be content to be discontent,
> thou shalt be better in a little while,
> Thou shalt talk about the needy,
> thou shalt pray they make it through,
> Thou shalt thank the Lord you're not like
> them, thou shalt be orange and blue,
> Thou shalt settle down in quarantine in the
> land of the '*thou shalt nots.*'
> And everyone you have ever met will long for
> what you've got.
> Thou shalt not even enter a public house,
> thou shalt not turn water into wine,
> Thou shalt not question authority,
> thou shalt not put religion on the line,
> Thou shalt not mix with sinners,
> thou shalt not talk to prostitutes,
> Thou shalt not be in the world at all,
> thou shalt not be their substitute,

Thou shalt settle down in the trenches in the
land of the '*thou shalt nots*'.
And this talk of a radical Jesus is just some
Muslim, Buddhist, Communist, Humanist,
Socialist, Ecumenical, New Age plot."

Let me draw this address to an end; if you are a slave
and you want to become a son, or if you are a son and
you're living like this as a slave, here are the two things
that you need. You need to hear again and believe the
gospel. It's wonderful just to hear the gospel. I was so
greatly rebuked by one of our members from a Roman
Catholic background . . . rebuked because we did not
celebrate communion every Sunday. He said, "You know
if you miss a particular Sunday in a Presbyterian church
you might not have communion for a year." I was greatly
rebuked by that because I could be preaching through
some passage in the Scriptures that may not necessarily
have a reference to the cross and to the gospel. He said
that at least in Mass there was a focus upon sin,
atonement and forgiveness. I was so rebuked, that every
Sunday now in Lucan there is at least one point in the
service where I declare the gospel. I announce the gospel.
Often it is through a corporate confession of our sins
and I say to the people, "This is the gospel. No matter
what you've done, no matter who you are - if you really
believe, then there is forgiveness for you through Jesus
Christ." You need to hear the gospel and you need to
believe the gospel. Secondly, you need to open your
heart afresh to the Spirit of God to come and hug you -
just to hug you, and say, "You're my son! You're my

daughter!" And we will say, "And you're my Father!"

And so the Spirit will witness with our spirits, that we are the children of God.

"If the Lord has laid it on your heart to give £100,
I want you to stand"

Spirit not Law

Galatians chapters 5 and 6

An infamous American T.V. evangelist came to the U.K. and hired one of those vast auditoriums. Unknown to the congregation he wired up all the seats with substantial voltage and when he came to the climactic moment of the service he said, "If the Lord has laid it on your heart to give £100, I want you to stand," and he pushed a little button and everybody jumped to their feet. When the service was over, the stewards found twenty dead Scotsmen clinging to their chairs. Now we shouldn't be too hard on the Scots. They have every reason to be proud of their nationality and ethnic origin because you see, originally, they were Irish!

I think many of us will have seen that powerful Scottish nationalist film 'Braveheart'; interestingly, much of it was filmed within my Diocese! I have a parish, but really it stretches through much of Ireland and 'Braveheart' was filmed at Trim Castle. If you've seen the film you'll realise this is a violent and evocative film. It's a mixture of history and myth, focusing on this man called William Wallace. He led a campaign against the colonial reign of the English in Scotland. In the film, Wallace is captured and tortured, but even under pain of death he will not recognise the authority of a monarch from England in Scotland. At the climax of the film he's on the rack; it's a tense and dramatic moment and some of you will remember this. You see him writhing in pain and then Mel Gibson, who plays Wallace, fills his lungs to the maximum capacity and with the help of Sony-Dolby stereo surround, screams the one word '*FREEDOM*' and it resonates and reverberates through the cinema . . . but also in the hearts of men and women everywhere. In "Les Miserables", the musical version of Victor Hugo's book, there is this lovely song,

> "Do you hear the people sing,
> lost in the valley of the night.
> It is the music of the people
> who are climbing to the light;
> For the wretched of the earth
> there is a flame that never dies
> Even the darkest night will end
> and the sun will rise.
> They will live again in freedom
> in the garden of the Lord.
> They will walk behind the ploughshare,
> They will put away the sword,
> The chains will be broken
> and all men will have their reward."

It is, you see, the international cry for freedom.

When we are set free from something we are set free for something. Listen to Eugene Peterson: "Imagine, will you, a prisoner incarcerated for years in prison, now elated at his moment of release. He has spent a long time behind prison walls, his life has been completely controlled and regulated by the terms of his punishment - his clothes, his food, his sleep, his work, his recreation have all been dictated by prison officials. Then he is set free, he stands outside the prison walls with a new set of clothes, a little money and his freedom. The freedom is exhilarating. He has dreamed of this; now he's experiencing it - but he cannot stand there forever. He must do something with it." What are we to do with our freedom? We are free *from* something *for* something. The people of Eastern Europe, as you know, having been released from the oppression of totalitarian communism, now find themselves in the tyranny of nationalism and ethnic cleansing. Freedom demands constant and eternal vigilance.

Let us look at these marvellous words of the Apostle Paul, Galatians chapter 5 verse 1 following, **"It is for freedom that Christ has set us free. Stand firm, then, and do not let yourselves be burdened again by a yoke of slavery."** If you are a Christian, if you are a son of God, you have been redeemed from slavery, you have been set free from guilt. Contrary to Sigmund Freud, guilt is not a mere pathological condition; it is of the very essence of our humanity as men and women who are morally accountable to God. That is why Mark Twain says that humans are the only animals which blush and the only ones that need to. We are guilty, and from this guilt we have been set free; in addition we've been set free from self. By nature we are, in the words in Malcolm Muggeridge, "trapped in the dark little dungeon of our own egos." We are born that way;

you do not have to teach a toddler to say 'me, my, mine' - it just comes naturally to them. We are slaves of a fundamental selfishness and if you have been released you can sing,

> "Long my imprisoned spirit lay
> Fast bound in sin and nature's night,
> Thine eye diffused a quickening ray,
> I woke! The dungeon flamed with light!
> My chains fell off, my heart was free,
> I rose, went forth, and followed thee."

You have been released, liberated from self and you have been set free from fear - from the fear of death, the fear of judgement, the fear of suffering, the fear of the occult, the fear of superstition, the fear of mysterious powers, Christ has set us free. But free for what? **"It is for freedom Christ has set us free."**

These Christians in Galatia, and, I suspect, most of us, started off perfectly well. We experienced something of the liberating power of God within our lives and we enjoyed and were elated by that freedom but now we are in danger. The danger comes, as you have discovered in this letter, from those who are profoundly religious. Paul uses this wonderful imagery which we find in verse 7, of us running in a marathon or around a track. One of the other athletes, these Judaisers, who have come down from Jerusalem, they've cut in in front of us - you've seen this in a race; you may even have been at a meet and observed it. For the athletes all the rhythm, balance and focus has been destroyed; they begin to trip and some of them even fall, so that these Galatians find themselves lying on the track utterly confused.

Now it is important for us, as it was important for the Christians in Galatia, to understand who these people were and to recognise the evidence of these agitators who would drag us into bondage. In these verses Paul gives us some insight as to the sort of people we will encounter in our churches and in our Christian organisations who would seek again to enslave us. The first thing you notice is that when you hear what they say, it does not have the ring of truth as we read in verse 8, **"That kind of persuasion does not come from the one who calls you."** The sheep recognise the voice of the Shepherd but when you hear these people, even though it seems so appealing and persuasive and reasonable, there is something within your soul that says, 'There's something funny about this'. Now I know, because of my upbringing and background in Northern Ireland, that many of you have been brought up on a diet of this extraordinary cocktail of evangelical conviction, cultural identity, political aspiration and a commitment to a portion of land, the six counties which we call Northern Ireland - and you just have received it as a package deal because that's the way it is. But something has been happening to you, not just here but over a considerable number of months and years, which says to you, "There is something strange about this; it just doesn't hold together; it no longer has the ring of truth."

Secondly, your thinking and behaviour will be stifled by these sort of people. It will, says Paul in verse 9, be like a little yeast working through the whole batch of dough. These people, who seek to entangle you in a yoke of bondage, will sit with you on church committees, they will attend church meetings and when you are with them it's like playing that game on the radio, "Just A Minute". And it's as if they have that little buzzer in front of them and they're watching and they're waiting for any hesitation, deviation or repetition - the buzzer goes, Oh! and they're on to you like a flash. They have that utterly censorious judgmental spirit - the law drives them and they will easily entangle you in their bondage.

Thirdly, they will emphasise the external and the visible so that other people can see it. That's why these characters are obsessed with circumcision. Most of those who entangle us into slavery are obsessed with external things which are utterly peripheral - like communion tables. Should you move it in order that the young people can communicate the gospel more effectively? Should the pews be moved or not? Should we have an overhead projector in our church? These things, which are peripheral and secondary, become central because people like this are obsessed with the visible. What is even worse is when these people come to us and say things like, "There will be no blessing in this church until them women start wearing their hats. There'll be no blessing until those dangly earrings are removed. There'll be no blessing until the skirts get longer!'" Paul is extremely irritated by this, and by these characters behind it, that he is extremely crude here. You can't escape it, because these Galatian Judaisers were taking these new converts and seeking to have them circumcised. Then they were bringing them into the washrooms and the public baths in front of the other Jews and saying, "Look! Hey, this guy is one of us now!" Paul says, "If you really want to impress them, why don't you just get castrated? Be emasculated! That would be really impressive." It's rather crude, I don't deny that, but it's in the text and if you give in to such slavery the consequences are dire. Paul is saying that if you allow yourselves to be circumcised in order to be acceptable before God then you will have bought into a religion of law; and can I say, brothers and sisters in Jesus Christ, that you are on the path to slavery if you accept that anything else is needed except what Christ has done for you, received by faith alone. I know that it's extremely attractive to be drawn into these various movements and organisations because you need security, you need identity and you desperately want to do what God wants you to do. To make matters worse, people will come in the most subtle, insidious ways and suggest various things that they say are really absolutely necessary for you in order that God will bless you and that you might be acceptable before God.

I'm going to be quite direct in what I say now. If people come to you and say, "Look you must be confirmed by a bishop in apostolic succession in order to be acceptable before God and acceptable before us," *they are adding to the gospel*. If someone comes to you and says, "You must be baptised by us in our way in order to be acceptable before God and acceptable to us," *they are adding to the gospel*. If someone comes to you and says, "It is necessary for you to be baptised in the Holy Spirit and to speak in tongues in order to be acceptable before God and acceptable to us," *they are adding to the Gospel*. If someone says to you, "It is necessary for you to subscribe to the Westminster Confession of Faith as a confession of your faith, in order to be acceptable before God and acceptable to us," *they are adding to the gospel*. Of course I think it is valuable to subscribe to the Westminster Confession of Faith; I think its important to be baptised; I think it is necessary and wonderful to be filled with the Holy Spirit - but if anybody says to you that any such thing is *necessary* for your acceptance before God and before the fellowship of God's people, they are entangling you in slavery. That is the clear message of this passage and the result is dire. Paul says basically, 'You're on your own mate.' Look at chapter 5, verse 2 where Paul states that, **"Christ will be of no value to you at all."** In verse 3 he says that you must keep all the law, **"I declare to every man who lets himself be circumcised that he is required to obey the whole law."** He insists in verse 4 that your relationship with Jesus Christ is broken, **"You have fallen away from grace."** You're on your own from that point on; you'll be seeking to do your best according to the law with no assurance that everything is going to be all right ultimately. It is a dire life of entanglement to slavery. What is the alternative?

This is wonderful! It is the life of freedom and Paul describes it almost with a sort of holy nonchalance. He spells it out in Galatians chapter 5 verse 6, **"It is faith expressing itself through love."** The contrast between this and the oppressive bondage of all of those people who are seeking to heap laws and rules and regulations upon you is quite radical. It's like chalk and cheese. So, says Paul, we live by faith, through the Holy Spirit with the motivated hope of righteousness. We know that we are in the right even though we're in the wrong because Christ has done everything for us. That is why at the conclusion of Paul's argument in Romans chapter 8 you will find all these marvellous rhetorical questions that he hurls against the enemy. **"Who will bring any charge against God's elect? . . .Who is he that condemns? . . . Who shall separate us from the Love of Christ? . . . For I am persuaded that neither death nor life, neither angels nor principalities, neither things present nor things to come nor any powers . . . nor anything else in all creation will be able to separate us from the love of God which is in Christ Jesus our Lord."** This is the liberated hope of those who have been declared in the right even though they are in the wrong. And so we sing,

> "No condemnation now I dread;
> Jesus, and all in Him, is mine;
> Alive in Him, my living head,
> And clothed in righteousness divine.
> Bold I approach the eternal throne
> And claim the crown through Christ my own."

However, says Paul, this freedom that you have - faith expressing itself through love - is not a licence. Look at verse 13, **"You, my brothers, were called to be free. But do not use your freedom to indulge the sinful nature; rather, serve one another in love."** You know from your own experience that there is a civil war going on within you between the old nature (i.e. the sinful nature) and the Spirit (i.e. what you have become). A new creation has taken place within you. You now participate in what Paul calls 'the new mankind', the totally new order of things. But these desires are in conflict and the war which you have experienced is unremitting and relentless. Now what is this sinful nature that is sometimes called the flesh? I have a great respect and admiration for Saint Augustine; he is one of the great heroes of the Church - not least against Pelagius. Augustine re-discovered the doctrines and the nature of grace. But poor old Augustine had major problems with his sexuality; major, major problems. And Saint Augustine identified the flesh, the sinful nature, with his normal, natural, sinful appetite. Now that has had a dire effect upon the Western Catholic Church, including Protestantism, so that when we consider the sins of the flesh, the things that we immediately focus upon are in terms of our sexuality. This is wrong. Our sexual appetites are as natural as needing to go to 'the loo', or wanting to have a glass of water. That is something we have been born with. God has given it to us as a gift. The problem arises when these natural appetites and desires are controlled and governed by the self, by the ego; at that point they become the lust of the flesh.

What happens to us when we choose to act according to our own selfish desires, when we become egocentric? Paul tells us, and here is the list in verse 19 following. When you get into your sinful nature, says Paul, this is what's going to happen to you.

Your sexual choices will be based entirely upon your natural desires, sexual immorality, impurity and debauchery. I have my hair cut - not too regularly because it's so expensive – but when I go, it's to Peter Mark's! When you go into Peter Mark's there is this colossal poster which says, "If it feels good, do it." Well, of course, that is the philosophy of our contemporary culture; in terms of our sexuality, whether you are heterosexual or homosexual, that's the way you are born; your natural desires must be fulfilled and satisfied and you end up, as Paul describes it, in immorality, debauchery and sexual perversion.

In terms of religion, you begin to use spiritual powers, even the living God Himself, if necessary, as a resource to get what you want. That is part and parcel of our culture is it not? Paul described it as idolatry and witchcraft. We are in control, you see, and that is why, today, people are profoundly religious and spiritual. It is a reflection of the New Age phenomenon in which you draw upon all of these spiritual forces, energies and powers . . . even the little people. Fairies are back. Did you know that? I know of someone who talks to her fairy; the fairy tells her what to do and how to behave; she draws upon these spiritual energies and resources – it's a form of idolatry - in order to achieve what she wants to achieve. There are some people, even within evangelical churches, who respond to God Himself like that. The epicentre of their lives is not the living God, but they themselves are at the centre and so they draw upon God to assist them to do whatever they want to do. That is the lust of the flesh, says Paul.

Socially and relationally these people are totally obnoxious. How would you like to be married to someone like this – someone who shows hatred, discord, jealousy, fits of rage, selfish ambition, dissension, and so on? Who could live with someone like that? And yet that is what people are like who are governed by the lusts of the flesh, by the sinful nature; they are totally undisciplined in their lifestyles. Look at the last part of the list (verse 21), **"drunkenness, orgies and the like."** They have no control over themselves in their consumption of drugs or their use of language. Have you noticed how someone's language deteriorates when that person's 'self' is in total control? And the two areas in which swearing predominates are the two areas concerning the most intimate aspects of our humanity - our sexuality and our relationship with God. It's indiscipline you see.

The opposite of this is, of course, the Spirit. He is the one who makes us truly human, and you can sum up the fruit of the Spirit in one word, love. Let me give you a definition of what I mean by love. I have worked with this definition in Lucan for many, many years:-

> "Love is an act of the will whereby we seek the good of another and in doing so sacrificially give ourselves away."

Love is not a feeling. It's an act of the will whereby we seek, not the happiness, but the good, the 'summum bonum' of another, and in doing so - like Christ who sacrificed Himself for us, we sacrificially give ourselves away. Paul says that the fruit of the Spirit will be manifest in love in these ways and John Stott very helpfully divides this description into three triads. As the fruit emerges in our lives God-ward, or upward, it will express itself in love, joy and peace. As it emerges man-ward, or outwardly, it will express itself in patience, kindness and goodness; and as it emerges self-ward, or inwardly, it will express itself in faithfulness, gentleness and self-control.

Now let me say something to you: if you are a child of God and His grace is at work in your life there is something within you, even as I give you this list, which says, "Yes. I want to be like this; this is what I have been created for; this is what I have been redeemed for, but how can I achieve it?" Let me say this to you quite clearly – the law cannot achieve this. It cannot legislate for this. It cannot create this. This is not the fruit of the law. This is the fruit of the Spirit. Now, of course, in the history of the Church various attempts have been made to impose law in order to create righteousness. During the medieval and monastic periods of the Church, and of course we have the hangovers from that period to this day, there are those within various orders who take vows - vows of chastity, vows of celibacy, vows of poverty and vows of obedience. Their intention is that, through conformity to these laws, they might develop the fruit of the Spirit, a life of holiness. Some have even gone to the extremes and used forms of flagellation. You've seen this on television or in books where people will take things and literally whip themselves until blood begins to pour down their backs in order to evoke some sense of holiness or godliness within them. In the 1930s, in the Protestant churches, there developed a movement called 'moral re-armament' led by Frank Buchman, a man of genuine intent, who was concerned at that stage with the moral malaise of society. He began to articulate absolutes to which he expected people to conform - absolute purity, absolute unselfishness, absolute honesty and absolute love. Let me assure you that even with all those absolutes and vows it is impossible to produce this fruit. It is only possible by the Spirit.

In the context of this civil war that is raging within us, between the flesh and the Spirit, how do we deal with that which is naturally perverse and how can we encourage that which is of God? I believe that the two key words which explain Paul's argument here are the two words *attitude* and *action*. Look at verse 24, **"Those who belong to Christ Jesus have crucified the sinful**

nature with its passions and desires." What he is saying is that if you are a Christian through the cross of Jesus Christ your sinful nature has already been dealt with. That appetite, controlled by the self, has already been nailed to the cross. The war is over. What we're involved in now is a mopping-up operation. If you are to live with the *attitude* that, "I have already been crucified with Christ," then it will require *action* on your part; we are to mortify the flesh. Practically speaking, it means we will not entertain or titillate those things that will be harmful and damaging to us. We will avoid reading certain books, watching certain programmes, participating in certain events; that's how we mortify the flesh. It requires action.

What about the Spirit? Again it requires *action*. Look at verse 25, **"Since we live by the Spirit, let us keep in step with the Spirit."** Those who are Christians have the Spirit of God within them already; God has taken the initiative. He prompts us, He urges us, He nudges us. You know something of what I'm speaking. One of my great concerns as I handle the Scriptures and seek to expound the word of God, is that people will hear what the Spirit of God is saying to them through the Scriptures.

We believe that the Bible is God-breathed. Now what we mean by that is what you are engaged in when you chat and talk to all sorts of people. You are breathing - but you are breathing in such a way that air is moving over the larynx, over the voice box and it's creating words and you are communicating - your breathing and your speaking are inseparable. We hold this Book to have such authority because God's breath causes him to speak His word. That's how it was at creation. Do you remember the creation narrative? God's Spirit is moving over what he has created. Even though it is in chaos, at the same time He is speaking and it is done. As the scriptures are handled, as they are taught in the power of the Holy Spirit, God speaks.

> "And His that gentle voice we hear soft as the breath of even,
> That checks each fault, that calms each fear, that speaks of heaven.
> For every virtue we possess and every victory won
> And every thought of holiness are His alone."

He's doing something, isn't He? He is at work, that's the action.

In the light of this, what *attitude is required from us? I was brought up in a tradition - and you may be familia*r with this and you may still embrace such a view - that says when God begins to do this for you and in you, your response is to let go and to let God in which you are essentially passive. That is not the teaching of this passage. The attitude of the Holy Spirit within us requires action in order that the fruit of the Spirit might emerge. What I am suggesting to you that if the Spirit of God has blessed you and ministered to you and done something within your life, you are not to say to yourself, "I have had this extraordinary experience, this fuzzy, warm, indescribable experience of God. Now where is the next conference that I can go to? Is there one on next week, or the following week, or next month? That degenerates into what we call a type of spiritual narcissism, an obsession with ourselves, in which the experience becomes a resource for our benefit. When the Spirit is at work, He requires action, practical action. Here are the four things you are to do, all of which are recorded in chapter 6.

The four ways we are to keep in step with the Spirit are:-

First, you are to restore those who are fallen – chapter 6 verse 1. It's a lovely picture of the fishermen mending their nets by Lake Galilee, or a doctor setting a fracture, or returning a dislocated bone to its place. When those who live by the law are confronted by those who have fallen, what do they say? They say, "They've made their own bed, let them lie in it. Let them stew in their own juice." The response of those who are governed by legalism is to do nothing or to say, 'We have our standards to maintain', or, 'Let's make a public example of them'. But those who are in step with the Spirit show such empathy and gentleness that Paul says they even put themselves into danger in order that they might restore them. I have such a dear friend; I love him to bits. He is married, but he has foolishly become involved with another woman. Now he's broken it off and we are working our way through all that has taken place - it's just hellish. But we're seeking to restore him as we walk in the Spirit. Do you know the name James Bakker? James and Tammy Bakker are a laughing stock in the United States. They were T.V. evangelists with their own T.V. station called 'P.T.L.'. Then they got themselves into all sorts of a mess; their marriage has broken up, he was involved in an affair and financial corruption . . . but he was a Christian - *is* a Christian. He was incarcerated in prison for years, guilt ridden, oppressed, lonely, isolated. He has written his story and he's working very humbly now among the poor because he thinks that's appropriate. He doesn't want to have a public profile, but in his book he tells how one day as he sat in his cell in a state of utter depression he received a message that there was someone there to see him. He was absolutely amazed, as he hadn't had any visitors at this stage, because nobody wanted to have anything to do with James Bakker. So he went out into the reception area and there standing in front of him was Dr. Billy Graham. Bakker says, "I put my head down, I was so ashamed," and Billy walked forward and just put his arms around me and hugged me. *THAT* is walking in the Spirit; that's keeping in step with the Spirit.

Secondly, Paul says, if you're in step with the Spirit you will **"carry each other's burdens." (Galatians** chapter 6 verse 2) Jim Packer has this lovely quote in his book, 'Keep in Step with The Spirit': "Modern Christians tend to make satisfaction their religion. We show much more concern for self-fulfilment and for self than for pleasing our God. Typical of Christianity today, at any rate in the English speaking world, is its massive rash of 'How To . . .' books for believers, directing us to more successful relationships, more joy in sex, becoming more of a person, realising our possibilities, getting more excitement each day, reducing our weight, improving our diet, managing our money, licking our families into happier shape and what not. Granted they spread a thin layer of Bible teaching over the mixture of popular psychology and common sense they offer, but their overall approach clearly reflects the narcissism, selfism or 'me-ism' as it is sometimes called."   I was in a bookshop once and I saw these marvellous books for Christians who were on diets. They had titles like, 'Trim for Him' or 'Firm Believer' or how about 'I must Decrease and He must Increase'! In contrast, those who are in step with the Spirit are not obsessed with these things. They are more concerned with carrying each others' burdens. I want to say something about the backroom people in your church – the people who make things happen, but never look for any kudos - the people who do all those little tasks and you always wondered who on earth did them. Do you ever affirm and encourage them? These are wonderful people. These are Spirit-filled people. Do you get what I'm saying? Those who are walking in the Spirit carry each others' burdens.

Thirdly those who are in step with the Spirit engage in radical self-evaluation. They really know themselves. Galatians chapter 6 verse 3, **"If anyone thinks he is something when he is nothing, he deceives himself. Each one should test his own actions. Then he can**

take pride in himself, without comparing himself to somebody else, for each one should carry his own load."
Listen to this little ditty I found: –

> 'Sometime when you're feeling important,
> Sometime when your ego's in bloom,
> Sometime when you take it for granted
> You're the best qualified in the room.
> Sometime when you feel that your going
> Would leave an unfillable hole,
> Just follow these simple instructions
> And see how it humbles your soul.
> Take a bucket and fill it with water,
> Put your hand in it up to the wrist,
> Pull it out, and the hole that's remaining
> Is the measure of how you'll be missed.
> You may splash all you please when you enter,
> You can stir up the water galore!
> But stop - and you'll find in a minute
> That it looks quite the same as before.
> The moral of this quaint example
> Is to do just the best that you can.
> Be proud of yourself . . . but remember
> There is no indispensable man!

I had a lovely experience with a lady in our church who I call 'the philosopher of Lucan'. I was running around like a headless chicken; I had this to do and that to do, and she said, "Trevor, what's wrong with you?" So I began to go through this colossal list of things that were my responsibilities and duties, and she said, "Trevor, I wouldn't bother if I was you, because when you're dead and gone we won't even remember that you've been". I think, perhaps, the Holy Spirit gives us a slightly more affirming and positive estimate of ourselves. What does the law do? It makes you *pretend*, doesn't it? By comparison and contrast, you have to think that you are better than you actually are or you're worse than you actually are. But the Holy Spirit, like a jeweller (that's what this verb means) examining a precious stone, estimates your worth and your motives and you come to know yourself. You develop a true estimate of yourself so that you can get on with it - you just get on with the work. Some of you may think that I have been rather critical of people from Northern Ireland, but let me assure you one of the great strengths of Ulster is the thranness and stubbornness of the people. That really is a wonderful asset, especially if you're a missionary. I remember a director of one missionary organisation saying to me, "Give me an Ulster girl any day! There are some who come to me and they're wondering 'Do I have the right gifts? Am I being fulfilled? Is God's blessing on me in this place?' And this wee Ulster lass from Co. Armagh or Co. Antrim is in there up to her uxters, going flat out because she knows herself and she just wants to get on with it and God blesses those people." The people like that who we have in our churches are just pure gold.

Finally, if you're in step with the Spirit, you are exceedingly generous to those who minister the Word of God. Listen to this, **"Anyone who receives instruction in the word must share all good things with his**

instructor." (Galatians chapter 6 verse 6) If you live by the law, which is rampant in this country, north and south, what does it mean in terms of finances and giving to the work of the Church? Well, it makes you utterly miserable. It is like paying your taxes; you give as little as you can to get as much as you can, don't you? That's the law. But those who are walking in step with the Spirit they just give with utter abandonment, no big deal. When I was in Bangor I received a marvellous letter from a lady who always called herself my 'Wee Granny'. She wrote,

> "Dear Trevor,
> You might have wondered at getting a cheque addressed to you for £67.99, but this was the amount I saved up and was going to use to get a black all-wool coat. I'm not able to walk around shops now, so I had to get it through the club. I had bought no coat for three years and I told myself that I needed this one, until I heard your message this morning. Then the Lord said to me, 'Do you really need to buy this coat when you already have two or three other coats that will last you quite a time? You don't go to functions, so that money could be used for the work of the Kingdom of God.' So here it is. I'm not by any means rich in this world's goods, but I'm able to pay my way. After first giving the Lord what is His share, I give a lot of money to my personal friends with different missions, but I always feel all our money should be used as the

Lord leaves, for if He owns us all, that includes
all our money - and I want him to own all of me.
Thank you for the blessing you are to me,

Your Wee Granny.

Isn't that great?! £67.99. Some of you could write a
cheque for £6,700.99 and not even miss it, but this
woman is in step with the Spirit. It is a principle of
harvest, that what we sow is what we reap. Paul writes
at the end of this section, that if you sow to the old
nature, you'll reap destruction; if you sow to the Spirit
you will reap eternal life.

Now I am going to close with this final section (chapter
6, verses 11-18) and I don't want you to miss this,
because here the cross holds everything together that I
have tried to bring out of these chapters. That's why
Paul takes his pen from his secretary at this point in
the letter. He takes it from what we call his amanuensis,
the person who has been receiving the dictation, and
he writes in large letters. This may have been because
of arthritis, or possibly because his hands have been so
badly bruised and beaten by suffering for the gospel, or
it may be because of the ophthalmic condition that
many commentators think he had. Whatever the reason
was, he writes in large letters for emphasis. It's his way
of saying, "Whatever else you've missed, don't miss this."
And he writes in these large letters, "You have a choice,
circumcision or the cross."

In the first talk I explained to you that the passion for

circumcision among these Judaisers was all about identity. This was the thing they gloried in, they boasted in it. They believed it was necessary for Christians to become Jews and conform to the regulations and obligations laid upon the Jewish people in order that they might celebrate their identity. Now, says Paul, these characters are putting you under pressure to be circumcised so as to avoid suffering for the cross. Remember there was this resurgent Jewish nationalism; the Zealots (the paramilitaries of that time) were functioning in such a way as to force people to conform, or suffer the consequences. Paul says, "You know what's happening. They want to make a good impression among their Jewish friends in the public baths. They want to be able to show that Gentiles who believed in Jesus, had to become one of 'their own'. They want to say, 'It's great to believe in Jesus as Saviour and Lord, but you have to become the same as us'. What they boast in as most important of all, is their identity." Then Paul writes these glorious words, **"May I never boast except in the cross of our Lord Jesus Christ, through which the world has been crucified to me, and I to the world."** As good evangelical Christians, we know that it is through the cross that our redemption has been secured and that sin has been dealt with. But what we have failed to perceive in this country is that the cross has dealt with this issue of identity, which has torn us apart. The cross not only deals with the vertical, it deals with the horizontal too.

At the beginning of Paul's letter to the Galatians he

speaks of how the cross has rescued us from this present evil age (Chapter 1 verse 4); now he speaks of the world. By **'the world'**, by **'this present evil age'** he means to depict the tensions that exist between Jews and Gentiles, between unionists and nationalists, between Celts and Brits. Paul says that the cross has so dealt with this tension that I boast, **"in the cross of our Lord Jesus Christ, through which the world has been crucified to me, and I to the world." (Galatians** chapter 6 verse 14) The consequence is that neither being a Jew nor a Gentile, circumcision or un-circumcision means anything. You can be a unionist, Brit, nationalist, republican, loyalist; you can be a Presbyterian, you can be a Roman Catholic – it means nothing in terms of ultimate salvation. **"What counts,"** he says, **"is a new creation." (Galatians** chapter 6, verse 15) You see what Paul is saying is that through the cross he is now part of a new order of things. He now lives as a child of the age which is to come.

Let me ask you, are you part of this radical new order, this new mankind, this new society, the Kingdom of God, the new creation which has been achieved and accomplished through the cross of our lord Jesus Christ? *That is what matters*. Then Paul adds, **"Peace and mercy to all who follow this rule, even to the Israel of God." (Galatians** chapter 6 verse 16) What peace and mercy we would experience in this land and in our churches if this rule governed our country and our people! As Christians we would not only turn the world upside down; we would turn it the right way up.

Let us pray: Lord it is so great to be your child, to be a son of God. Forgive us that we have been so easily entangled with slavery. We ask that only those things that we have heard from Your word that are in accordance with Your will and purpose will be implanted in our hearts and minds, and those things that are peripheral or contrary to Your truth may be forgotten. Take this gospel and cause it to set us free, through Jesus Christ, Our Lord Amen.

Bibliography

George, Timothy:
Galatians: A new American Commentary, Broadman & Holman, 1994

Hansen, G. Walter:
Galatians: The IVP New Testament Commentary series, IVP, Leicester, 1994

Longenecker, Bruce W.:
The Triumph of Abraham's God, T & T Clark, Edinburgh, 1998

Longenecker, Richard N.:
Galatians: Word Biblical Commentary, Word, Dallas, Texas, 1998

Longenecker, Richard N.:
The Ministry and Message of Paul, Zondervan, Grand Rapids, 1971

Luther, Martin:
Galatians: a revised and completed translation based on the 'Middleton' Edition of the English version 1575, James Clarke & Co. Ltd., London, 1953

Meara, Mary Jane Frances Carolina:
Growing Up Catholic, Doubleday, New York, 1985

O'Brien, Conor Cruise:
Ancestral Voices, University of Chicago, Chicago, 1995

Packer, James I.:
Keep In Step With The Spirit, IVP, Leicester, 1984

Peterson, Eugene H.:
Travelling Light, Helmers and Howard, Colorado Springs, 1988

Postman, Neil:
Amusing Ourselves to Death, Methuen, London 1985

Stott, John R.W.:
The Message of Galatians, Only One Way, The Bible Speaks Today, IVP, Leicester, 1968

Swindoll, Charles R.:
The Grace Awakening, Word, Dallas, Texas, 1990

Wright, N.T.:
Justification; 'The Biblical basis and its relevance for contemporary Evangelicalism' in The Great Acquittal: Justification by Faith and Current Christian Thought, ed. G. Reid, 13-37. Collins, London 1980